# TIREE

## *War among the Barley and Brine*

Mike Hughes and John Holliday

THE ISLANDS BOOK TRUST

LIVING HISTORY
THE ISLANDS BOOK TRUST
URRAS LEABHRAICHEAN NAN EILEAN

Published in 2012 by The Islands Book Trust

**www.theislandsbooktrust.com**

ISBN: 978-1-907443-38-1

Text © Mike Hughes and John Holliday
All photographs © Mike Hughes unless otherwise indicated
Cover images © Parker, Gill, McKinnon and Roberts

The Islands Book Trust would like to thank Bob Chambers and Donnie Morrison
for their help in the production of this volume.

The Islands Book Trust, Ravenspoint Centre, Kershader, South Lochs,
Isle of Lewis HS2 9QA. Tel: 01851 880737

Typeset by Erica Schwarz
Cover design by Raspberry Creative Type
Printed and bound by Martins the Printers, Berwick upon Tweed

HIE
**Innse Gall**
Outer Hebrides

# Contents

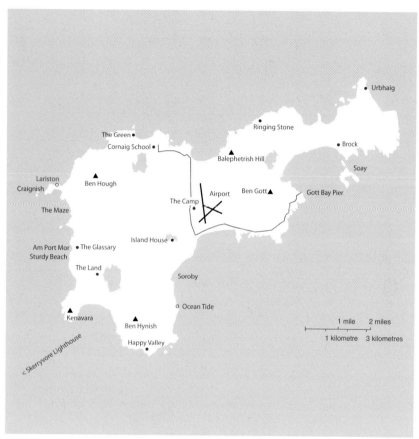

Map, showing main townships on the Isle of Tiree. (Woodcock)

The Green •
Cornaig School •
Ringing Stone •
Balephetrish Hill ▲
Urbhaig •
Brock •
Soay
Lariston
Craignish °
Ben Hough ▲
The Camp
Airport
Ben Gott ▲
Gott Bay Pier
The Maze
Island House •
Am Port Mor
Sturdy Beach
The Glassary •
The Land
Soroby
Ocean Tide °
Kenavara ▲
Ben Hynish ▲
Happy Valley •
< Skerryvore Lighthouse

1 mile 2 miles
1 kilometre 3 kilometres

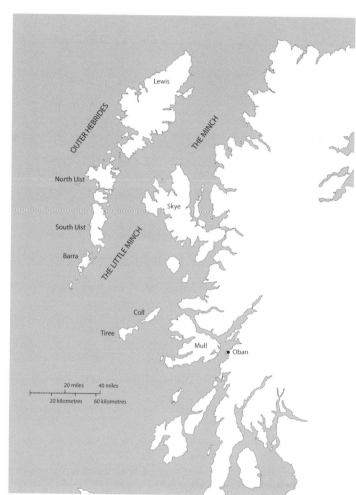

Map of west and north Scotland and the Hebrides. (Woodcock)

Lewis
OUTER HEBRIDES
THE MINCH
North Uist
Skye
South Uist
THE LITTLE MINCH
Barra
Coll
Tiree
Mull
Oban

20 miles 40 miles
20 kilometres 60 kilometres

# Introduction

I am a very fortunate man. Not just because my family tolerates and assists me in this, my research hobby. I am also fortunate that my wife Barbara's mother is from Tiree and her father from Taynuilt. This has not only brought me into close contact with the lands of the north and the west, but more importantly – much more importantly – it has given me friendship with islanders such as the Maclean, Mackinnon, Campbell and Munn families, along with many, many others of the most generous spirit and character. It also began my quest for the stories of the servicemen who were posted to this island, and their kindness and warmth has humbled me.

Tiree attracts me so; surrounded by a shimmering sea, a land where bountiful barley was grown and milled, with centuries of tales and fairytales shared with visitors, by gentle folk linked in name to forebear or locale.

The Second World War was a time when sacrifice and self-sacrifice were the norm – not easy concepts to comprehend in the twenty-first century. Duty, faith and love of

The Battle of the Atlantic. The longest and perhaps most crucial battle of WW2, fought across millions of square miles of ocean. All sorts of vessels were pressed into service to help keep Great Britain and her Allies in the war. Tiree was one of a number of forward air bases on Scotland's west coast which were vital in efforts to counter the U-boat threat. In the foreground of this photo is HMS *Campbeltown* (with censored number). This ship went on to achieve great renown in the 'Raid on St Nazaire'.

country were unashamedly the predominant perspectives on life. Young (and not so young) Hebridean men and women flocked to the Merchant Navy, Royal Navy and Highland regiments. And at home the islanders did not just 'dig for victory', they 'crofted to conquer'. I ask myself every day – are we truly worthy of that generation's legacy?

Did the war ever really leave Tiree? Perhaps the marram grass covering the sand dunes still murmurs the secret stories of these times, while the sea ebbs and flows, rises and falls. What might the inquisitive visitor learn from these shores, from the quiet, unhurried thoughts of a courteous but unyielding islander?

I am so grateful to John Randall for the opportunity to publish this book. What a pleasure it has been to share the task with Dr John Holliday. In the pages which follow we try to harness something of this tumultuous time. Where possible, we allow islanders and visitors to tell their own story. Several of the wonderful people who shared their insight with the writers are no longer with us. It is our fervent desire that a little of their spirit lives on in these pages.

*Mike Hughes, Bellshill and Balemartine, August 2012*

Off-duty airmen relaxing among Tiree's sand dunes. Jim Green and friends, groundcrew, Tiree, 1942. (Green)

In October 2010 Tiree stood still as we remembered the terrible events of 1940 on the rocky shore of Sandaig. One of those leading the ceremony to commemorate the stranding of HMS *Sturdy* was Mike Hughes, who has assembled an encyclopaedic collection from this period of the Highland's history. I suggested to him then that he should write up his Tiree notes, and it has been a privilege to work with him on this.

The Second World War was a pivotal turning point in the island's story. Over the years *An Iodhlann*, Tiree's historical centre, has made many recordings of the oral traditions of the island, including memories of the Second World War. It has been an honour to work with these tradition bearers and I hope we have done justice to the poetry of their stories.

*Dr John Holliday, Balephuil, Tiree, August 2012*

# CHAPTER 1

# The Gathering Storms

Tiree before the Second World War was very different to the Tiree of today – and very different from the mainland. This was an island without mains water or electricity, where crofting was powered by horses and the fishing boats by sail, and where Gaelic was the almost universal language of daily life. An island remote from the mainland, yet with strong family ties to Glasgow, Canada and New Zealand.

The Atlantic was one of the key battlegrounds in World War Two. The Royal Navy, the Merchant Navy and RAF Coastal Command all paid a high price to keep Britain supplied – one estimate is that 12 million tonnes of Allied shipping went to the sea bed. On the German side 500 U-boats and their crews perished. With the east coast and southern ports more vulnerable to Luftwaffe raids after the fall of Norway and France to the Nazis in the spring of 1940, the North Atlantic became Britain's lifeline. While the First World War was a mostly distant conflict, the second raged close to the Hebrides and western Scotland.

Many features of both World Wars were foreseen by John MacLean, Tiree's most famous seer. *Iain mac Eachainn Bhàin* was born in Ruaig in the early nineteenth century. Most of his life was spent as a shepherd at Hough, a large farm in the north-east of the island. Concerning the coming wars he said the following:

> 'Listen to me and give ear to what I say. There is a great war coming soon, such as the world has never seen. There will be a great battle and thousands will fall in one day. In addition to that, many soldiers will be injured and wounded when a white smoke will come down. In the Atlantic Ocean, narrow iron vessels will travel underwater, letting loose narrow silver fish that will blow the large vessels to the bed of the ocean. On sea and land the losses will be heavy and in a land which is unknown to me, the ground will be soaked in blood. Millions will go to their eternal rest in the soil of this land and beautiful red flowers will grow over them.

Mrs Dolina McCallum, Crossapol, obtaining water from a well. This traditional method was still much in use during and after the war. (Davis)

These dark days will pass over for a time, with new devices pouring arrows of death from the sky. Millions will perish during this disaster. Tiree will undergo many great changes. Many armed forces will come to the island. They will live in strange houses and large birds will rise up and lie down on the plain of the Reef. Steering these strange birds will be people with noses like pigs' snouts'.

News of the war reached the island.

'We had an old radio set that crackled and banged and we actually heard the broadcast, "Consequently we are now at war with Germany." I remember it well. The mood was very sad. Very, very sad.' Angus Munn, Heanish

'I remember the day the war started as well as today. And, I'll tell you, I was coming from Kenavara, well it poured with rain, and I've never seen rain like it before or after. It was a Sunday, and every place got dark with this rain. They were at church down

Tiree family group, photographed just before the war. (J McKinnon)

at Balemartine, and nobody was in the house. When they came back, they got word that the war started. People were terrible frightened, especially old folk, and young folk as well. They were talking about the old war, the 1914 one. That's what it was'. David McClounan, Balephuil

'It was a very hot summer that year 1939. I remember it well, and war was imminent, and thinking, "What's going to happen now? It's only twenty years we've had a war already, a very disruptive one and all." It was on a Sunday it was declared, 3 September, and do you know this, you would think that the heavens had opened, or hell, the day we had here with thunder and lightning. And all through that day, I remember it very well, neighbours calling.

'The following morning my stepmother went into the room where I was sleeping and she says, "I've just heard from Hugh MacKinnon, that the Athenia has been torpedoed after leaving Belfast last night". I remember that well. "My God!" I said. "I knew that boat. I wonder if there was anyone there that I knew." I was very worried about it.' Hugh MacLean, Barrapol.

The SS *Athenia* was the first maritime casualty of the war. Bound for Canada, she was struck by a torpedo and 112 people drowned. On board were Tiree seamen James Downie, from Ruaig, sailing as first mate, and deckhands John MacDonald and Neil MacLean. All survived the tragedy but the war had arrived on Tiree's doorstep.

As early as September 1939, a 'D Notice' had been placed on Tiree, making it an offence to publish information about the island without prior authorisation. Tiree became a 'Restricted Area'. Permission to travel to Tiree had to be sought and was only granted to those who could prove they came from the island.

Plans were soon made to build an aerodrome on Tiree and contractors hired.

3 January 1940: "The Air Ministry are proposing to acquire land on Tiree for the purpose of establishing a bombing and gunnery school." [National Archives Scotland – Department of Agriculture]

Land on The Reef was requisitioned, some from crofters who had been given their land in return for service in the First World War.

Cathie (MacLean) Forbes of Heylipol, in NAAFI uniform. (Campbell)

*'I worked in the contractor's canteen at Crossapol for over two years. The navvies and the Pioneer Corp had a camp nearby. Girls from Tiree, Barra and other islands who worked in the canteens lived on the site but my father would not let me, so I stayed at Paterson's farm. My brother was at sea and later this helped me to get into the WRENs.'* Margaret (Campbell) Kennedy.

16.1.40 letter from REC Johnson to the Air Ministry: *It is possible that prehistoric remains might be exposed when the ground is being levelled and this Department [Office of Works] will request the Air Ministry to inform us immediately if any remains are encountered.*

A letter from A Page, the Chamberlain of the Duke of Argyll, Inveraray, 16.4.40: *The Reef, together with other and lesser lands in Tiree was requisitioned formally...by the Air Ministry... cattle will require to be considerably reduced. With regard to sheep stock, it is anticipated that this will require to be cleared entirely...The outlook for the holders is decidedly gloomy on the face of it all.* [National Archives of Scotland]

Tiree crofter at work ploughing. (Holleyman)

'Melville, Dundas and Whitson, a Glasgow firm, had one of the contracts to build the airport on the Reef at the start of the war. The company were digging gravel from the Sturdy beach and a party with Whitson and an Air Ministry official went to inspect the work. An Irish digger driver was sunning himself beside his cab, while the lorries were off to the airport, when he was meant to be greasing the machinery. "Who do you work for?" asked the official. "Melville, Dundas and some other feckin ass!" replied the man. MDW was known by us as "Men Don't Work". Alasdair Sinclair, Balinoe

'Over at the drome there they started digging up a lot of the ground, they started building hangars – that's the first thing they did. And then they started making runways, and big lorries came in, and they were taking it over, you know these big round stones. That was for the foundations. There were boats coming in, puffers with tarmac, that was going on top of these founds. They took tons upon tons of stones out the beach at West Hynish.' David McClounnan, Balephuil

'The first part of RAF Tiree built was the control tower, the old control tower. It's knocked down now. And then they started building the runways. There were quite a lot of Tiree people working there, and Uist and Barra people. Irish people were there too. Suppose you went to the moon, you'd get an Irishman! They had camps both sides of the road [in Crossapol], towards MacLeod's shop. You couldn't see that place for camps. There was a post office there and everything.' John George MacLean, Scarinish

Tiree men, working the fields in the 1940s. (D McKinnon)

A pier was built on the beach of Tiree's north shore. This 'Road to Balephetrish Pier' was part of a national undertaking initiated by Winston Churchill in May 1942, to test the potential for getting troops and equipment ashore quickly [on piers which could withstand tidal surges].

'We were told the Balephetrish pier was built as part of a series of experiments to see which design of piers, on sandy beaches, were best, as part of the preparations for the Normandy landings. They intended to build a railway from there to the aerodrome.' Hector MacPhail, Ruaig

The pier collapsed in a matter of days, after an Atlantic gale.

# Early Days of RAF Tiree

As the authorities deliberated on Tiree's eventual role in this world war, slowly and steadily young men began to learn that they were being posted to what must have seemed, at best, an unexpected location. For some it was to be an endearing experience, and they made the most of the initially spartan conditions for servicemen. For others the relative isolation was not at all to their liking.

Bill Singleton was one of the very first wartime 'visitors' to arrive on Tiree in 1940. While the Battle of Britain was raging elsewhere, the Battle of the Atlantic, in fact the very struggle for Britain's survival, was just taking shape.

Men of Number 31 RAF Embarkation Unit, being photographed outside a Nissen hut at Scarinish pier. (Dimond)

*'We had two Nissen huts and a workshop at the pier. We sometimes had ceilidhs at the RAF base at the pier.'* John Nielson.

'I spent three months on Tiree and I think it must have been the happiest days of my life. I was sent there as a LAC electrician. I caught the boat in Oban on a beautifully calm day when one could see the wake stretching out for miles behind. On Tiree I found a company of three airmen manning a small radio station in Scarinish, billeted in a private cottage. It actually transpired that the Post Office had built a repeater station on the island but the RAF had to provide someone to man it. This was in readiness for the aerodrome, which was in the course of being planned and constructed. I was billeted in a farmhouse in Scarinish, drawing my rations from the local store and Post Office, who always seemed to have a 'wee something extra' each week.

'There wasn't a pub or cinema on the island, and friends could not understand how I could be so happy there. What they did have though were dances in the village schoolroom. These would not start until about 10.00 pm and would go on until two in the morning. With most of the young men having enlisted in the forces, and the RAF not being there in any numbers, men were in the minority, and the ladies decreed every dance after the first was a "Ladies Choice." What a boost to one's ego!

John Nielson, a hardy Lanarkshire farmer, volunteered for service in the RAF. He demonstrates the qualities displayed by young men in this 'time of emergency'. 'I was with the Embarkation Unit (EU) at Scarinish for two years from 1941. There was also a Maintenance Unit at Scarinish and later air sea rescue launches. Before being posted to Tiree many of us had worked for a time at the Great Western Hotel, Oban, (RAF) garages.

'The RAF commandeered a Mrs MacKenzie's house [Bank House] in Scarinish and we had a workshop behind it. The Unit was about 30 men and 18 vehicles. Flight Lieutenant Waghorn was our CO. We also helped to repair the vehicles and the ASR launches. When HMS *Sturdy* ran aground, and when RAF planes crashed, we took the bodies to the pier before they were taken away on boats. Courts of Enquiry were held in Scarinish School.

'My time on Tiree, in fact my life, was almost cut short. I was driving to the Reef from Scarinish one evening, coming to a small bridge over a stream [at Baugh]. A Melville, Dundas and Whitson construction lorry was coming the other way and did not stop. I hit the brakes, (they did not work) on my Bedford Tanker. I hit the wall, broke through

Members of No 31 Embarkation Unit (with John Nielson second right) outside the 'Banker's House', Scarinish.

*'On Tiree we were billeted with civilians in Scarinish and Gott Bay, including Mrs Anderson and Mrs MacKenzie. We had meals with Mrs MacKenzie.'* John Nielson.

and hit the bank on the far side of the stream. I believe I was rescued by two teachers out walking. The next thing I remember is waking up a week later in Killearn Hospital. Captain Barclay of Scottish Airways probably saved my life. He answered the emergency call, even in terrible weather, and flew me to Glasgow. My friend who was with me in the cab died. After ten weeks in hospital with a fractured skull, broken leg and broken arm, I was offered my discharge papers from the RAF. I refused, and returned to Tiree.'

Percy Williams was to find many surprises on his first RAF posting. 'I'm originally from Swansea in South Wales. I served on Tiree, Isle of Islay, Benbecula and Barra with the RAF, Number 10 Construction Squadron. I did my basic training at Blackpool. Then I was posted to Tiree in 1942. My service on the isle was most educational. The work I was doing, building runways and roads, was not. The people of the isles were, and are, wonderful people. I was only 18 at the time and somewhat homesick. There were four of us all posted together, all new members of the RAF, wondering what type of aircraft we would work with. But my arrival at Tiree was a time of despair. I thought "What have I come to now?" Windy, rough wind, rain and cold rain! Along the roadside were posts

Tiree from the air in 1942, looking in across Soroby Bay and Crossapol. Many of the recently completed RAF accommodation sites are clearly visible. Tiree had in fact previously known 'military occupation' within, what for some elderly islanders would have been living memory. In the 1880s a force of Marines had spent time on the island in response to 'Land League reform' protests. (Clark)

with rope nailed to the top of the posts. This was to assist us in walking along the road to the cook house.

'The following morning I found my first job in the Royal Air Force – making breeze blocks! We were met by a Sergeant and a Corporal, and a dirty lorry with signs of cement, earth etc. I said "What unit are we joining? What type of planes?" "Planes?" he said (he was not a nice guy). "You're not going to be anywhere near planes. This is a construction unit!" All four of us were completely downcast. We were of the General Duties (GD) classification. About 80 per cent of the boys on our new unit were from Glasgow. I, having had sheet-metal work experience, volunteered at seventeen to be a Flight Mechanic Airframes. There was an air field, and it had Coastal Command Liberators on it, but I did not have anything to do with them.

'One of my mates had wireless (radio) experience. After a few weeks he became withdrawn from the happy fellow he had been. "I must go to the wireless room," he would say. "I am on late duty today." We did not even have a wireless to listen to during the evenings. He would walk off the job, off to nowhere. The NCO in charge would get really upset. Finally he was put on CO report. Thank goodness the CO realized there was something seriously wrong with this airman. The Medical Officer (MO) was sent for. That was the last I saw of him. We finally got word that he was sent back to the mainland to a military mental home. (I later learned he was discharged, and I believe recovered from this experience).

'I experienced a lovely relationship with the crofters. There was never a closed door to me, maybe because I was the only Welshman in the unit and known as "Taffy". I remember speaking one day with a remarkable older person (eighty-year-old) – born, lived and never had left the Isle of Tiree. He wanted to know all about Wales. He was very interested in me speaking Welsh. We were not known as Air Force but as the "Royal Egg Force". One of the reasons for that title was that when anyone went on leave they would take as many eggs home as they could carry, and butter also.'

(Authors' note: Percy did eventually get to work on aircraft and there are still a number of those WW2 breeze block structures standing on Tiree today, almost seventy years after Percy and the other young men constructed them. Not bad work, considering that was by no means their first choice occupation in the services).

Bob Spinks had the job of feeding the growing RAF station. 'I was LAC Cook/Butcher in the advance party to open the RAF station at Tiree in November 1941. Our CO on Tiree was Group Captain Tuttle who had his own Spitfire. When I was there he used to fly around the island. There were about 40 men in the advance party. This grew to about 2,000 with about 40 WAAFs when the Hudson and Liberator aircraft arrived.

'I remember Scarinish very well. I spent a week up there in a cottage, cooking for a wireless unit. The army units on the island were the Cameronians and the Royal Pioneer Corps.

'I can remember the ferry was unable to reach Tiree in 1942 for over a week as the weather was so bad. So we had no bread and had to have corn[ed] beef and biscuits for a few days. I can well remember having to jump from the jetty at Tiree on to the deck of MacBraynes *Lochearn* in rough weather.

'For the first few months we had to use the bath and showers on the labour camp till ours were finished. Our boxing team were matched against a team of civilian workmen on the island at the time. I remember we lost every bout that evening! The work men were a tough lot, mostly from Glasgow.'

Hugh Hunter has fond memories of Tiree which lasted all his life. 'I was one of the initial airmen sent to Tiree and our address was known as *Port Mòr*, where a few stayed

Men from RAF Port Mòr, on Balevullin Beach, 1941. (Hunter)

*'We walked across fields to get to work. I liked Tiree – it was so lovely in the summer, wild flowers and lovely sands. Tiree's wild flowers were the best I have seen. I used to walk down to Balemartine to the post office and also watch the fishermen. Once I went to a dance in a small hall near our station, dancing Scotch reels and Strip the Willow.'* Bob Spinks.

*'We soon moved to our permanent site at Kilkenneth, which were Nissen huts. When the contractors started to build there the islanders informed them that, during the winter months, where the huts were being constructed was a pond. That turned out to be the case and my Nissen had water from end to end for a short time. We had to step straight into wellingtons when rising.* Hugh Hunter. (Hunter)

in a house in that area and others in a bell tent. I was a corporal in the RAF. There were a small number of naval personnel in Scarinish when I arrived on Tiree. I was on Tiree in 1941 and stayed there for about 16 months. Apart from the enjoyable periods, some airmen and soldiers could not settle happily. We had one soldier determined to get off the island. He put a rifle to his foot and shot a hole through it. He was on the boat off the island, very shortly after that, and also on a charge.

'Our washing facilities were tins filled with water from the streams. It naturally had to be boiled before being used for cooking. On one occasion the sergeant in charge of transport, Monty Banks, decided to try and wash in the sea. Two airmen out walking saw him and they picked up his clothes, leaving only his shirt and boots, and left him to walk nearly naked past whatever croft houses there were, to get back to camp.

'The winds on occasions were hurricane force and our cookhouse, which was one end of a Nissen hut, was blown away, with all the pots and pans. Walking in the darkness was far from pleasant as corrugated metal sheets, waiting to be erected into Nissen huts, were often blown from one end of the island to the other. Eventually we had electric power and water supplies. Conditions were then appreciably improved.

'During one stormy period we had ships wrecked off the island on two consecutive nights. One was a tanker destined for America [the *Lariston*]. We assisted in the crew's rescue and in appreciation they gave us the contents of their larder, when they got back on the vessel. This consisted of meat, such as we never got ourselves. Also a large cask of rum, which came at the same time as our issued barrel of beer (we got one of those about every 4–6 weeks). The mixing of the beer with rum created havoc, and the ones that indulged in this mixture all passed out completely and had to be carried to their beds!

'We had practically no stores in the early months and we had only one issue of clothing when I was there. The ones we had were in a terrible condition as we only wore our best uniform when going on leave. When we rescued the crews from vessels none of them could credit that our untidy bunch were actually RAF.

'While I was on Tiree it was said that a party of girls of "ill-repute" endeavoured to come to Tiree from Glasgow but were not allowed to land. From all accounts they had heard the civilian contractors were making good money, but could not spend it when on the island.'

Jim Green is less enthusiastic about his days on Tiree than some. 'I do not look back with pleasure at my time on Tiree but souvenirs, memories and friendships provide a certain amount of pleasure and nostalgia. I was a mere clerk in Station HQ, with not an aircraft in sight except Group Captain Tuttle's Auto-Gyro that he used occasionally to leap across to Glasgow. Yes, I was mostly unhappy. I was a young London lad of nineteen years and my previous posting was to Station HQ in Blackpool, with all its colour and noise. Tiree was a horizontal rain-slashed, windswept island, in what appeared to be the middle of nowhere. I loathed going back after leave and the long journey.

'I remember the four gallon petrol can we used to fill from an adjacent burn with its brown coloured water, and place overnight on the heater in the hut so we could shave with a little warm water.

'I started as dogsbody to the Station Warrant Officer and was promoted to Station Engineer Officer's clerk. I spent day after day amending aircraft engineering manuals. What a bore! After a few months I was detached to Group HQ in Liverpool. This was more like it for me, living in the middle of town and surrounded by three or four members of the WAAF. Alas this was not to last. After a few more months I was returned to Tiree.'

Philip Bridge recalls, 'I enlisted in the RAF on 10 May 1941, and was designated Clerk GD, and therefore was not involved with anything technical or flying duties. After "square bashing" at Skegness and Boston (Lincolnshire) I was posted to Tiree in the late summer of 1941. I had never been to Scotland before and the train journey and sea trip to the island has remained with me to this day. On arriving at the island I found I was one of the first airmen sent there. We had one officer, Pilot Officer Samuels, billeted at the Scarinish Hotel, I believe. We also had a NCO and a cook among our 20.

'At this stage our living accommodation was three Nissen huts – a dormitory, a cookhouse and a store – situated well away from the airfield itself. The ablution building was only four walls and a roof with no doors or windows, and the plumbing was non-existent!

'Some of our chaps were invited to a dance and enquired if there was a band. The answer was in the affirmative, but it turned out to be a solo fiddler. Even so, I think they all had a good time.

'We had a Polish squadron for a short time. The pilots seemed to be quite mad. It was said that when the squadron moved on, the planes dipped so low over the "farewell party" that they were forced to lay full length on the runway!

'We ran short of supplies once. A ship had arrived on Sunday and pier workers would not unload on that day. It was sorted out in the end, and we got back to our proper meals.'

# HMS *Sturdy*

For the Allies October 1940 was a terribly bleak point in the saga of WW2. Invasion of Britain was a distinct possibility, with the USA more than a year away from entering the fray, and the Soviet Union eight months. Vital support from key allies – Canada, Australia, New Zealand and others – was on its way, but it had to travel across thousands of miles of hostile ocean. The convoy system had been introduced, but Britain was desperately short of escort vessels and the U-boats were beginning to take a terrible toll in the north Atlantic. The war was about to arrive with a sickening thud on the stormy shores of Tiree, in the shape of hideously twisted metal and lifeless bodies flung up on the beach.

HMS *Sturdy*, registration number H28, was built by Scott's of Greenock and had been launched in 1919. She was a 1,000 ton 'S' Class destroyer, with 3 four-inch guns and 4 torpedo launchers. Before the war she had been modified to carry mines.

Harry Springett, who sailed on the boat, remembers. 'She was generally in a bad state of repair and, looking back one wonders how we ever kept her going. She leaked just about everywhere and during bad weather life on board was atrocious. There was no hot water system.'

The *Sturdy* was under the command of 31 year old Lt Cmdr George Tyndale Cooper. He had joined the Navy ten years previously and had been marked down for accelerated promotion. It was his first command and he had been the captain for little over a year. Two of his fellow officers on board were just 20 and 22 years old.

Harry Springett had joined the Royal Navy in 1933 as a boy sailor. He became part of the destroyer's crew in May 1940 as a Leading Seaman. 'We had a lot of mature sailors, reservists. Lt Cmdr Cooper was not popular with the crew and was often seasick.'

On the 26th of October 1940 HMS *Sturdy* had left Londonderry to join convoy OL9 off the Northern Irish coast. The next day Cooper was ordered to meet another inbound convoy, SC8. As the weather deteriorated with a gale from the south and enormous seas estimated to be 30 feet high, the *Sturdy* started to run low in fuel and was pitching and rolling badly. Lt Cmdr Cooper decided to make for port. Unable to take radio bearings and disoriented by the weather, in the early hours of 30 October the captain spotted what he thought was a line of surf on his port side. Moments later there were three sickening crashes and he knew they had hit rocks. The *Sturdy* had in fact hit Tiree – a reef off the gravel beach in Sandaig, now known as 'Sturdy Beach'.

Harry Springett remembers, 'When we ran aground on Tiree it was at the end of a terrible convoy, with many ships lost. It was a vile night, no visibility. At first we thought we had been torpedoed.'

The captain ordered 'Slow Astern' but he could tell by the vibration of the boat that the situation was hopeless and that the screws were hitting the rocks. He therefore gave orders to abandon ship and for a distress signal 'Aground on North West coast of

HMS *Sturdy* photographed early in WW2.

*'She was generally in a bad state of repair and looking back one wonders how we ever kept her going. She leaked just about everywhere and during bad weather life on board was atrocious. There was no hot water system.'* Harry Springett.

Ireland – or Tiree' to be sent. The crew gathered on deck in the dark, wind and rain. For the next half hour, until water got into the fuel tanks, the engineers managed to keep the power on, and the forward searchlight picked out some low lying land. Believing the ship was breaking up, Petty Officer Rickards was one of two men who volunteered to swim to the shore to set up a line. When they reached the beach Rickards followed a cart track until he reached some houses. There was no answer at the first house but at the second a woman opened the door.

'These first sailors had come to the door of Mairi Morrison's thatched house. She was at home with her sons Lachie and Alasdair. It was a frightening sight as the sailors were covered in oil and it was pitch black.' Effie MacDonald, Middleton

A Carley float was now launched from the destroyer but the swell dashed the sailors on to the rocks. The officers decided then to launch the large whaler, manned by thirteen crew. This too capsized and two sailors were lost. In all, five young men drowned on the shores of Tiree that terrible early morning.

At this point the crew saw a flashing light sending a message in Morse code. 'On no account attempt to leave ship' followed by another, 'the tide is falling.' The tone of the signal seemed so authoritative that the captain decided to follow the instructions. Captain Donald Sinclair (*Dòmhnall an Dan*), who sent the signal, was home in Greenhill on leave from the Merchant Navy. He had been wakened and had hurried down to the shore with a torch. His action saved many lives. Cruelly, Captain Sinclair was to die himself in the Atlantic on his next voyage, when his boat, the *Empire Eland*, was torpedoed.

Harry Springett continues, 'I was coxswain on the whaler and volunteered to go ashore. As soon as we hit the water we were swamped by waves, we were thrown into the sea and many were dashed on the rocks. I found myself swimming beside two young sailors. I could hear one begging the other to let go. He had a "death-grip" on his neck, as he could not swim. We were all so close, he could have grabbed me. They both drowned and I was eventually washed up on the shore. I could see a sailor in the sea. It was Samways, a friend, and we did all we could to drag him onto higher ground, but we were so exhausted. I lay there, I don't know how long, then a crofter appeared almost as in a dream, and lifted Samways into a wheelbarrow and took him to safety.

HMS *Sturdy* with her back broken, on the shore, near Sandaig, October 1940. (MacLean)

*'Hugh went onto the wreck to look for souvenirs with a couple of friends. Opening drawers they pulled out a bottle of whisky. The men were desperate to open it then and there but Hugh said, "No We've got to get off by Breeches Buoy and it wouldn't be safe with a dram inside you." So they took some cups and sat on the shore and had their dram!'* Sarah MacLean.

*'Later, horses would not go past the* baca *(sand dune) where Hugh and Willie pulled up that first body from the Sturdy.'* Donald MacLean, Oban (son of Hugh MacLean).

'I tried to walk, but my feet were badly cut by the rocks. Suddenly there were islanders assisting us and taking us to their crofts. Before long I had a hot bath, a beautiful bed and a blissful sleep. I believe the locals got the ship's rum. They deserved it!'

Quick to arrive at the scene were the MacLean brothers from nearby Barrapol.

'It was a Thursday, I remember it well. My brother Willie must have heard something moving outside, something being blown by the wind. This would be about 6 or 7 o'clock in the morning. It was quite a rough morning and it was raining – I would call it force 9–10, a severe gale. Just before we got down there [to the Sandaig shore] we could make out it was a naval vessel – the paint, the colour, you see. There were a lot of people there. You'd hear "Help!" The wreck would be about 60 yards from the gravel beach on the rocks out there. The first thing we met there – a body, a beautiful, young fellow. I picked him up and took him beyond the reach of the ocean and put him on the grass. And I remember I cursed everything, I cursed even God. I'm being honest with you.' Hugh MacLean, Barrapol

The destroyer quickly broke in half before the storm abated. The wreck held provisions that were too tempting to ignore for war-hungry Tiree. Angus MacLean, Scarinish, recalled, 'I never saw so much tea in my life.' He saw an old man from West Hynish at the wreck. He held the pockets of his old tweed coat open and someone literally poured the loose tea into them. 'It would have done him for a year!'

'It wasn't very safe. It's a wonder to me no one was hurt or even drowned. I was there myself looking for souvenirs, and for tobacco. My goodness, tobacco! Cigarettes by the million! Rum if you wanted it, plenty of rum too. And some of the boys [the Navy salvage party] would pinch a drop for a person, too!' Hugh MacLean, Barrapol

Mairi Campbell, *Corrairigh*, remembers the first Crunchie bar ever she ate came from the wreck (they had been invented in 1929).

One survivor, Stoker Albert Gallier recalls that after three days being looked after by Tiree folk, the crew were taken by ship to Oban, where they had to sleep on the restaurant floor in the Caledonian Hotel, before getting a lengthy train journey to Portsmouth, still in the clothing they were rescued in.

The chief engineer of the *Sturdy* had fractured his knee during the evacuation of the boat. His thirteen-year-old son, Mike Gibson, was sent to Tiree to collect what personal possessions he could. 'I do remember the hospitality and consideration that I received. I was treated as a guest, put up at the local hotel and transported out to the wreck site. The salvage party looked after me well. Some people, who lived in a nearby cottage, had collected all the sailors' personal belongings that they could find, and were holding them carefully against collection by the owners. I did collect some things of my father's from them.'

At a subsequent inquiry into the grounding, Lt Cmdr Cooper was found to be negligent. His punishment? Half pay for six weeks. One of his commanding officers wrote, 'The Captain committed an error of judgement, which was excusable in very difficult circumstances.'

Another commented, 'An officer of this calibre can ill be spared at the present time,' [reflecting the lack of experienced naval officers at that desperate stage of the war].

After the inquiry Cooper was transferred to HMS *Exeter*. In 1942 this cruiser was sunk by the Japanese in the Java Sea and he spent the rest of hostilities as a prisoner of war. He was later awarded the OBE for his leadership in the camp. He returned to the Navy, eventually retiring as Captain in 1957. [In one of those neat twists of history, the Medical Officer who did his retirement medical was Surgeon Commander Murdoch Brown, from Mannal, Tiree].

Over 50 years later Hugh MacLean in Barrapol had a surprise visitor, a man from Northampton. He introduced himself as the brother of a sailor who had died trying to get ashore from the *Sturdy*. Hugh took him down to the beach, where the vessel had grounded, and described what he had seen. 'I told him about the body and there was one thing I noticed about the dead man – he wore a civilian waterproof coat, not the navy one at all – and he had a gold ring on his finger … with a square on it. 'Is that the ring you saw?' asked the man, 'Oh, my God.' It was his brother Ordinary Seaman Rivett we picked up. That altered my way of seeing life completely, man's inhumanity to man.'

# George Holleyman

O ne 'incomer' to Tiree in wartime was not only fascinated by the Hebridean culture he encountered but lovingly documented the island and its people with a trained eye.

'In January 1941, at the age of thirty, I was called up and reported to the RAF Recruiting Centre at Blackpool. After ten days of being "kitted out" – inoculations, vaccinations, "pep" talks, lectures on patriotism and security, and receiving the rank of AC2, I was moved on to No.7 Recruiting Centre, Morecambe. I was given an identity card bearing particulars of my physical idiosyncrasies and my photograph. I had, in fact, become an RAF "erk". We drilled, stripped for physical training on the beach in

George Holleyman next to a standing stone near Moss, Tiree. (Holleyman)

Arctic winds, attended lectures, fired rifles and were taught the elements of service law and behaviour. In other words, we were "genned up".

'My papers said I was to be trained for the RAF Service Police. On 28 February 1941 I left Morecambe on a special troop train and after a long and tedious journey arrived at RAF Manston in Kent. Manston was one of the famous Fighter stations of the Battle of Britain. When I arrived most of the hangars and many of the buildings were still in a ruinous condition from the heavy bombing raids of the previous September. In the two months I was there we were attacked several times by German fighter-bombers, which generally flew in low, just after dawn.

'I was destined to go on to the Island of Tiree. On 17 August I was again on the move with a posting to RAF Kilkenneth via Dollar, Clackmannanshire, HQ of No.72 Wing. The Wing was the administrative centre for a series of radio location stations dotted across central Scotland, from Anstruther in the east to the Isle of Barra in the west. One of the reasons why so many radio location stations had been built along the western coasts of England, Wales and Scotland was that it was believed that when Germany attacked Britain, it could be via Ireland.

'From September 1941 to June 1943 I was on Tiree. The personnel were housed in the Nissen huts at Kilkenneth on the west side of Ben Hough. The three radio location stations were situated at *Am Port Mòr* [Sandaig], Barrapol and on the summit of Ben Hough. The RAF compliment comprised a Fl. Lt Commanding Officer, one or two technical officers, three or four sergeants and other ranks – altogether about eighty men. There were no WAAFs at this time. Attached to our station at different periods we had detachments of the Cameronians and the Royal Corp of Military Police.

'I had a special reason for being somewhat excited at the prospect of visiting the Hebrides. From 1930 I had played an active role in archaeological excavation and research in the county of Sussex. The leader of our team of amateur archaeologists was Dr Cecil Curwen, whose work had won him national and international recognition. He had taught himself Gaelic and would sing Gaelic songs, accompanying himself on the *clarsach* or Celtic harp.

'I had a fair amount of time as guard duties on a station which was not at first operational was a lonely business. The service policeman, armed with a revolver, generally knew when the service personnel and the rare visitors were expected. I therefore procured a Gaelic grammar and reading book, and gradually learnt to read and write the language, and could sing Gaelic songs and hymns. With the help of a bicycle I was able to explore the whole island.

'Many of the townships were served only by very rough roads, or just muddy and sandy tracks. Food rationing was part of the way of life in 1941–3, and for many years to come, so one of the attractions of island life was the comparative abundance of eggs, home-made butter and even locally made cheese. This was a way of getting to know the local inhabitants and obtaining entrance into their homes. As there were no towns, villages or pubs such as we have on the mainland, many of the airmen rarely left the station in their spare time, but others got to know island families and received much true Highland hospitality.

'I therefore soon made friends with quite a number of crofters of both sexes and was able to learn a great deal about their social life and the economics of running a croft. Small modern houses could be seen in most of the townships but my estimate was

A Tiree woman working on her croft in the shadows of Ben Hough.

*'I visited* Bella Mhate *(Isabella Maclean). She lived on a croft in the township of Kilmoluaig. Her cottage had an earthen floor and all her furniture, including her box bed, was locally made from driftwood. She was an expert cheese maker and used a stave-built perforated wooden press called a* fiodhan *and a metal press anchored to a heavy stone [now in* An Iodhlann, *Tiree's historical centre]. Bella derived her income from a herd of six cattle and a flock of about forty sheep.'* (Holleyman)

that two thirds of the population was still living in the traditional Hebridean thatched cottages, or similar cottages in which the thatched roof had been replaced with asphalt or a bituminous roof of some sort. It was also fairly common to see that, where a modern house had been built, the old cottages had been retained to serve as barns or byres and were still in good condition. They were without windows or chimneys. At the time of my stay on the island the indigenous population was estimated at about 1,450 but it was much enlarged by service personnel and imported labour from the mainland and Ireland.

'Many of the men had been in the Merchant Service and had spent long years abroad and most of the women had been "in service" on the mainland. No group of senior citizens could have lived more comfortably on their meagre pensions than these retired islanders, who had come back to spend their last days on Tiree. There was no electricity, no gas, no cinemas, no pubs and no dustmen, but life was safe, simple and cheap.

'The war had brought some unexpected benefits to crofters. There was the sale of surplus eggs, butter and cheese, and the benefit of an occasional lodger, as well as literally "gifts from heaven" in the form of Government grants of seven shillings & sixpence (7/6d) per head for mountain sheep, and £2 an acre for growing potatoes. Many of the crofters owned horses and carts and the contractors working on government projects, such as airfields and roads, would hire a horse, cart and driver for the fantastic figure of £1 a day. To airmen earning £2 to £3 a week this seemed a fortune.

'Although in size and structure the cottages were completely standardised, there was considerable variation in the furniture content and attempts at decoration. Walls were rough plastered and/or lined with wood. In most cases they had whitewashed wooden ceilings. Wooden walls had either been painted or lined with wallpaper. The division of the interior into a living room and bedroom space varied from one cottage to another. Furnishing comprised a wooden table, a few kitchen-type chairs, a wooden bin for storing flour called a *gèirneal*, a wooden chest, generally covered with a plaid, and in some cases an armchair on either side of the fire. The fireplace generally consisted of a small iron kitchen range in which wood or coal was burned, and on the top was displayed a large iron kettle and a *grideal*, or girdle, for baking scones. Oil lamps provided the illumination and most people had Tilley lamps, but hurricane lamps were handy if you wished to visit the byre or barn at night.

Balevullin township during WW2.

*'An 18 acre croft could offer a passable living for a small family, with between 2 and 5 head of cattle, 10 to 25 sheep and its acre of potatoes, supplemented in some cases by fishing. The crofters paid their rent annually to the Duke of Argyll's factor.'* (Holleyman)

'One of the best preserved cottages belonged to Mary (*Mairi*) MacLean, standing in a croft in the township of Balevullin. There was a circular well about twenty feet away from the front door, the water being pumped up by hand. The living room was simply furnished but with signs of sophistication such as window curtains, framed pictures on the walls and a case full of books. Mary still possessed her mother's spinning wheel and one stone of a rotary quern for grinding corn was still in the garden. Near the front door was a *cnotag*, or large stone with a basin-like recess, in which barley or seeds were ground. A wooden mallet was used for the process.

'A Mistress MacNeill showed me several lengths of cloth neatly folded and in excellent condition which had been made on a hand loom by her mother. As far as I could ascertain no loom had survived or was in use in 1941–3. Most of the lengths were dyed in coloured stripes, but others were monochrome in brown or mauve-like shades. I was told the dyes were vegetable and locally made.

'Clothes were passed on from one child to another and constantly patched. Shoes and boots were costly possessions, worn as little as possible and not at all in the summer. As the boys grew up they had to find sleeping accommodation in the barn or other outhouses. As the croft could not support large adult families, most of the children, on leaving school, had to go to the mainland to find employment. Tiree children had a good academic record.

'One day an airman on the unit told me he had found two horn spoons on a small rubbish tip (or midden) in the township of Balevullin. I used to visit an old couple, a brother and sister, at Urbhaig at the extreme east end of the island. Isabel (known locally as *Iseabel na h-Urbhaig)* had been in service on the mainland most of her life. She explained how the Gaelic speaking tinkers, or gypsies, who travelled from one island to another in former days, would call at a croft and ask for cow horns and coal. They would then light a fire and make the spoons.

'A Miss MacDonald lived at Sandaig in a well-preserved thatched cottage. She was then about seventy and lived with a brother of about the same age. I was fortunate enough to photograph her making butter in a vertical, stave-built, plunger churn. My discovery that primitive clay pots, called *cragain*, had been made on the island within living memory was published in *Antiquity* magazine in 1947.

'Crofters who grew cereal and potato crops used a simple single bladed plough drawn by one or two horses. I saw sickles, *corrain*, and scythes, *speala*, being used for reaping, but no tractors or power driven equipment. Kelp, or sea tangles, was used as manure, and at certain times of the year it was a common sight to see the crofters collecting these slippery loads with their horses and carts from the sandy bays. In each township there were two or three small sailing boats. Rock fishing was fairly common and the fish (saithe) was salted and pegged out on lines to dry.

'There were no specialist shops on the island, only a few general stores dotted about the various townships. Most of the women bought clothes by post from stores in Glasgow and Edinburgh. The general stores were regional centres for gossip and news. Here one saw money changing hands, but among members of the crofting community there seemed to be a great deal of borrowing and bartering which went on. Nothing was set down on paper, no notes or memos – just memory used. The system seemed to work, as I never heard of anyone being accused of dishonesty or not meeting their obligations.

Traditional croft house on Tiree, during WW2, in need of some repair. (Rackcliff)

*'A short distance from Isabel's house at Urbhaig was a ruined cottage, which had been occupied by an old lady when Isabel was young. Fifty yards away was a small rocky eminence, where the old lady said she had seen fairies and little men dance on mid-summer's eve.'* George Holleyman.

The 'Puffer' *Sea Light* (Ross and Marshall's), unloading coal at Greenhill, Tiree. (D McKinnon)

'Coal was delivered to the island by small, decrepit little steamships called "puffers" which dumped their cargo on the sandy shore. Intelligence of their arrival got around like magic (few crofters had telephones) and soon horses and carts were on the scene and the coal was transported away to the crofts. There were no bags, so how it was weighed and paid for, I cannot imagine.

'My two-and-a-half years in the ranks, which ended in June 1943 when I left Tiree, were very happy and I look back on them with pride, nostalgia and some amusement. In July 1943 I was commissioned and spent the next two years as a Photographic Interpretation Officer at RAF Medmenham in Buckingham. I lectured on Photographic Intelligence. My final job was Officer-in-charge of the Library of Air Photographs, taken by the RAF and the USAAF in all theatres of the war, comprising over seven million prints and half-a-million maps.'

After the war Holleyman returned to Brighton and set up a notable antiquarian bookshop while keeping an active interest in the archaeology of the area.

Today we are indebted to George Holleyman for his meticulous recording of what he saw, said and did while stationed on Tiree, and for his generous, gentlemanly character in sharing his precise memories. He died in 2004, aged 93.

# CHAPTER 5

# RAF Tiree Becomes Operational – 224 and 304 Squadrons

After a long struggle against 'the elements' to construct the airfield, the tempo of Tiree's war was set to alter in April 1942. Two RAF squadrons, complete with aircraft and dashing aircrew, arrived on the island – 224 Squadron, Coastal Command and 304 [Polish] Squadron, RAF.

## 224 Squadron

The intriguing tale of 224 Squadron, formed in 1937 as a reconnaissance squadron in Coastal Command, is not a routine wartime story by any means. It has been suggested that this squadron was 'banished' to Tiree, and given a chance of redemption there. In early 1942 there had been the disastrous episode of the 'Channel Dash', when German battle cruisers slipped through the English Channel past the RAF and Royal Navy. It seems 224 Squadron may have been sent north and made 'scapegoats'. This episode, and the famous '1,000 bomber raids' on German cities, may seem distant from Tiree's contribution to the lengthy Battle of the Atlantic, but that might not be entirely the case.

Joining the first operational 'draft' to Tiree was Sam Bagley. 'In April 1942 I was a twenty-one-year-old airman, who volunteered two years previously. I was an AC1 (Fitter Airframes). That is one of the unglamorous ground crew who helped to "keep 'em flying".

'Our boat journey from Oban involved about eight and a half hours in the old *Hebrides*. When we docked at Scarinish there was a whale of a job for we "erks" to do. There were a number of troops there, setting up radar stations and HQ. We were the first operational squadron to arrive, and, being a completely new aerodrome, everything needed for flying purposes had to be brought with us from the previous station – all the furnishings and fittings to equip the squadron offices, through to the heavy equipment needed for maintenance and service on the aircraft, including tractors, petrol bowsers, and tables and chairs for the huts. Things had already been manhandled on to trains, then off the train on to the boat at Oban then offloaded at Scarinish to lorries for the trip to Crossapol. It was hard work each time, but we were fit as fiddles and a friendly bunch of youngsters (mostly).

'Many of the locals were still a bit hostile to having any military at all, as it might bring the war a bit nearer. The belief that they locked their daughters in at night "just in case" gained a certain amount of credence. True or not, most of us stayed in, kicked a ball about, played cards, had a sing-song in the NAAFI, or simply lounged around on the beach.

'One of our pilot officers was trying to impress one of the WAAF establishment. One evening he borrowed a Jeep and took his lady to the far end of Crossapol beach. He got bogged down with the tide coming in. We were bundled, with tools, into transport vans and taken across the machair to the beach. The Jeep was just about down to the axles in the sand. We had to strip everything we could off the Jeep, and get it off the beach by a sort of chain gang. MT fitters put it together again. We understood that this "PO Prune" character was given extra orderly officer duties for his stupidity.

'About this time RAF Bomber Command had started its retaliatory raids on the German homeland, and I recall the euphoria and cheers that went up when the BBC news came on with, "Last night, one thousand RAF bombers raided Germany, dropping 'X' tons of bombs." The RAF wanted to organise another such "Party", but they couldn't find enough aircraft in Bomber Command this time. So they scraped together what they could, and that included a temporary transfer of 224 from Coastal Command to swell the ranks. This called for some hectic activity on all our planes. Each one had to have a special up-graded inspection by all maintenance branches, and then each one had to have its camouflage re-sprayed.

'The problem was that Coastal Command colours provided for all "earthward" surfaces to be sprayed duck-egg blue – easier to blend in with the sky when seen from the ground or from a U-boat. This would show up too clearly at night, particularly if caught in a searchlight. So all the aircraft had to be re-sprayed underneath. We ran out of matt black paint, and one officer authorised the use of some drums of black enamel paint. We could almost have shaved in the mirror-like surface that appeared as it dried off. (In fact, a pilot of one who got caught in a searchlight joked on his return that the enamel had saved his life – the reflected light beam had blinded the German ack-ack gunners and put them off their aim). We worked on the aircraft nearly forty-two hours without a hot meal. There had been a steady supply of tea and sandwiches, spam or snoek (ugh!).'

224 Squadron records show eleven aircraft and crews flew from Tiree to North Coates, Lincolnshire, and took part in the 1,000 bomber raid on Bremen on the night of 25–26 June 1942, before returning to Tiree. Many of their Hudsons were damaged by flak but thankfully there were no casualties.

Sam Bagley continues: 'The squadron then converted to Liberator aircraft and soon after we had an unfortunate occurrence. A crew had been sent out to meet and escort a homeward bound convoy. On the way they ran into a huge bank of thick sea fog, and for a time were flying "blind" (on instruments). Suddenly they flew into clear air and the convoy was directly below them. Unfortunately the naval gunners on one of the escort ships had heard a plane but could not see it. Not knowing whether it was "friend or foe" had opened fire the instant they saw it. A number of shells hit the plane, some exploding inside. Unfortunately one of the crew was attending to a call of nature on the Elsan [chemical] toilet and was, to put it mildly, caught with his pants down. He took quite a lot of the blast. The crew continued their mission until a relief plane took over. They landed safely but with a desperately injured crew-man on board, who died in the sick bay shortly afterwards. I was one of the party detailed to patch up the plane – a nasty mess – and the figure of about forty plus holes/patches goes through my mind.'

Andrew Hendrie, a pilot with 224, who went on to write some wonderful books about Coastal Command, served on Tiree for a short time. 'The airfield was hardly complete when we arrived, with initially no water supply to the ablutions. Water supply was a well just in range of our Nissen hut, but the water was of doubtful quality. On one occasion I heard a cry, "Can't you stop them?" I turned and saw one of the islanders – an older lady. "Can't you stop them – playing football on the Lord's Day?"

'Off duty times gave us the opportunity to explore the island, which to me was a largely sandy waste, interspersed with peat bogs and rocks. I recall a Highland breed doing its best to find some grass to eat – such a contrast to seeing herds of cattle in south-east England curling their tongues around lush pasture.

Joe Hunt sitting on an aircraft after 224 Squadron returned to Tiree, having taken part in the 1000 bomber raid on Bremen on the 25th–26th June 1942. (Hunt)

'A great diversion for off-duty aircrew was to visit a wrecked merchant ship where much of a day was spent in trying to launch one of its lifeboats that was half-filled with sand. Its emergency rations were still intact and comprised of cream crackers and Horlicks tablets.'

John Legg recalls, 'An American Navy pilot landed one day. He came from the US aircraft carrier USS *Wasp*, which was escorting a convoy some sixty miles or so from Tiree. His noisy single-engine plane circled our airfield and eventually landed, whereupon he climbed out, only to enquire, "Gee, is this Ireland?" Upon been told it certainly was not, he refused to return to his carrier without an escorting Hudson – to navigate the way!

'I shall never forget the beautiful silver sand of the beaches, the seals and the clear water of Tiree. Also the small coal-carrying ships which would run aground on the sand and remain for several days, delivering coal.'

As the war progressed, 224 Squadron went on to great achievements in anti-U-boat warfare elsewhere (a skill they developed at Tiree).

Liberator aircraft of 224 Squadron, which was stationed on Tiree in 1942. These very long range aircraft helped to close the 'Atlantic gap' on the U-boat. (Radford)

As Tiree first became 'operational' in 1942, a fascinating character became CO, Group Captain Tuttle, later Air Marshall Sir Geoffrey Tuttle OBE, DFC. Tuttle had taken a short-service commission in the RAF in 1925 and owed his early survival to the introduction of parachutes, becoming only the second man to bail out safely. When war broke out he had led the HQ section of the Advanced Air Striking Force to France. A year later he was appointed to head the Photographic Reconnaissance Unit, and later moved to Coastal Command on anti-submarine duties.

By 1943 Tuttle was commanding the anti-shipping wing of the Mediterranean, Allied Coastal Air Forces in North Africa. After the liberation of Greece he took charge of the RAF there and the Royal Hellenic Air Force. By 1946 at the age of 39, he was an Air Commodore, the youngest to achieve that rank. He retired in 1959 as Deputy Chief of Air Staff. During his career he flew more than 100 types of aircraft. At Tiree he used a Spitfire and, incredibly, an auto-gyro for personal flights. He died in 1989, aged 82.

Group Captain Geoffrey Tuttle in his office at Tiree. He is considering a map of Europe, perhaps before 224 Squadron's participation in the 1000 bomber raid on Bremen. (M Olizar, Sikorski Museum)

## 304 Squadron

304 Polish Squadron, RAF, was formed in England in August 1940 from Polish airmen and volunteers who had escaped Nazi occupation of their country. They initially served gallantly with RAF Bomber Command.

Sam Bagley (224 Sqn) 'I remember the Polish squadron arriving. The Poles had a reputation for being bent on revenge for the treatment of their land and people by the invading Germans. 304 Squadron had insisted on taking part in every raid possible until the powers that be finally decreed that "Enough is enough, you're going out to Tiree".

Edward Zarudski was a young pilot with 304 Squadron who tells us of the big changes the squadron faced at Tiree. We also gain an insight into the adventurous spirit that enabled these young men to escape German-occupied Poland and struggle their way across Europe to continue the fight, at first in France, then in Britain.

'When we came to Tiree (10–13 May 1942) our squadron was only up to half its strength of 16 Wellingtons and crews. The first quarter of 1942 was very bad. In that short time the loss of 8 crews and planes could not be readily replaced. This together with the growing intensity of the Battle of the Atlantic, were the reasons why this bomber squadron was posted to Coastal Command. It was a great change and challenge for us. We were trained to fly at night above 17,000 feet to bomb hardly visible targets from a great height. At first our planes still had their black war-paint on.

'At Tiree the operations were done in broad daylight at very low altitude (because at that time U-boat detection was mostly visual), using new to us, low-level bombing techniques. Tiree was a training place to learn quickly a new trade.

'I do have a pleasant recollection of the Hudson boys (224). Their friendly reception and the warm atmosphere of comradeship we experienced. A single outstanding personality comes to my mind – that of the Station Commander Group Captain Tuttle. He was loved and respected by all of us as an outstanding officer, superb organiser and a most winning personality. I still see his smiling face greeting us as we clambered out of the Wellingtons at the wind-swept aerodrome. I still remember how Group Captain Tuttle took us to the Officers' Mess in a very long Nissen hut and introduced us to 224 Squadron, with a suitable libation which followed. His thoughtfulness and hospitality

Rockall, under a heavy swell, photographed by the RAF during WW2. Rockall proved to be an excellent navigational aid. Winston Dimond's (518 Sqn) accurate navigation helped the Admiralty to re-position their bearings for this lonely Atlantic outcrop. (Hunt)

*'Our eyes were searching and looking for anything on the water. I remember once seeing on our way a small rock far in the Atlantic, waves crashing against it with a few seagulls and a little flag fluttering on it (Rockall).' Z Soleki.*

made our stay at Tiree memorable and when the time came to leave the islanders for RAF Dale in South Wales we did it with regret.

'Of the island itself I still have good memories. As a pilot approaching the airfield from north-west or south-east and using the three Bens as guides; the golden sands of Gott Bay; the craggy shores and the sea breaking on them; the brownish-grey rocks; the stone fences enclosing a few small fields still stand out in my mind's eye. In spite of the cruel westerlies in May and the classic "horizontal rainfall", the discomfort of living in draughty Nissen huts was not too great. We quickly got used to the island and eventually, we grew to love it. For Tiree truly was an enchanting place when summer came at last in June.

'My memory remains of sturdy, taciturn, yet kindly islanders, when we asked our way about or for an explanation of the unique Hebridean-house architecture. The tied-down thatched roofs without overhangs particularly interested us. For relaxation after flights one walked. We walked in pairs or in groups, along the rocky shores admiring the always changing sea. We climbed down some of the sheer cliffs on the north side, where the rock was rotten and tricky, to find seagulls' eggs [a nice soup – supplement to the diet]. With delicious Tiree kippers, they made royal breakfasts. It was worth the risk we took. Our quarters there, though primitive by Bomber Command standards, were comfortable and warm.

'From Tiree we flew towards Rockall and fanned out on anti-submarine patrols in the North Atlantic. When, occasionally, we could not land at Tiree aerodrome, we got

Hudson aircraft, shown protecting a convoy in a wartime advertising poster. This view looks from Fingal's Cave westwards towards Tiree. (Cunliffe-Owen)

diverted to Scotland or Northern Ireland. I remember one misty evening on returning from Aldergrove past the dark basalt columns of the Island of Staffa and hearing the "music" of Fingal's Cave resounding in my ears. We flew at sea-level almost, then.'

Edward Zarudski kept a chronicle and timeline of 304 Squadron's service at RAF Tiree in 1942:

'On 10 May the Technical personnel and first group of flying crews came overland and by boat from Oban, landing at Scarinish after a storm. The sea was agitated and many of the ground staff were sea-sick. Strong winds hampered unloading the gear and aircraft parts from the ship.

13 May – The operational Wellingtons are flown in from RAF station Lindholme. Extremely friendly reception by members of 224 Sqn. The squadron training in new operational procedures began immediately. Low level bombing exercises in Gott Bay and navigation at 1,000 feet altitude.

14–16 May – Winds, fog and rain slow down training.

17 May – More bombing and navigation flights. Strong westerlies.

18 May – 3 crews take off on 1st ops, 8 hours no-sightings. Planes returned with bombs (6 depth charges 250lbs and 2 x 250lbs bombs)

26 May – First attack on U-boat (crew of Sqn Ldr Buczma). U-boat was attempting to attack a convoy homebound. "Probable damage", the verdict of the Admiralty. 4 other crews had no sightings.

31 May – 7 Wellingtons on ops. One crew attacked a whale-shark! Another also attacked suspected U-boat but without results. Wellington (DV-781) ditched 300 miles NW of Tiree as a result of engine failure. The bruised and shaken crew spent 6 hours in a dinghy. Search planes from 304 and 224 finally located them and at 21.15 hours they were picked up by HMS *Boadicea*.

9 June – The crew of Flying Officer Hirsch spot submerged U-boat and attack it. Air bubbles and oil slick appeared. Admiralty's verdict: "probable damage".

15 June – After a great farewell party thrown by the Station Commander and the friendly 224 Sqn, 304 Sqn is transferred to RAF Dale.

'On the island of Barra at that time was the home of Mr Compton McKenzie. A mutual friend in London gave me a letter of introduction to him. One day I prepared our little Tiger Moth (squadron's liaison plane) for the sea crossing, with a fighter pilot's dinghy strapped to the wing (just in case). It was not far to fly. But when I got there the airfield of Scottish Aviation (the beach) was lined with anti-landing poles. I turned back and never visited the famous writer.

'I have many still lively memories of Tiree, the island where it rains horizontally. Both flying crew and ground staff left Tiree with regret, promising themselves soon to return to the beautiful and friendly place. But as far as I know, nobody ever returned. The war, and the post-war years, separated the Poles and the island they grew to love. But the memory of it still lives on in the hearts of the few survivors.'

The islanders have vivid memories of the dashing Polish detachment.

'We had hens and in the spring we would have eggs very often, although there was great rationing in the city for eggs. There were Poles here in the war. They had been in the air force and had got out before the Nazis came. They had broken English but were quite aristocratic, confident-looking. We would see them walking around the island. I remember them coming to our thatched cottage in Brock, seeing that we had hens around the place. My aunt went to the door, and these two Polish men clicked their heels and bent over and took her hand. They asked if she had any eggs for sale. My aunt was quite charmed with the manners they had, their graciousness. They got their half dozen eggs and she told someone else later that they were the finest body of men that she had seen!' Duncan Grant, Ruaig

Mr Z. Solecki has a less favourable perspective on this island posting. 'My recollection of Tiree is that of a bleak island with a few scattered houses and rocky roads to the quay. The sorties were very monotonous; all one could see was waves on the water. The Wellington carried two pilots, two air gunners, navigator and wireless operator/air gunner. Our eyes were searching and looking for anything on the water. I remember once seeing on our way a small rock far in the Atlantic, waves crashing against it with a few seagulls and a little flag fluttering on it (Rockall?).'

Mr Solecki is proud to record, 'With Bomber Command 304 Squadron lost 12 aircraft with 102 airmen killed, with 35 shot down and becoming POWs. During 304

Drawing by Holley Hughes

*'As boys we used to watch the bombers wheel over Vaul and swoop down low over Sgeirean nan Ròn in Gott Bay. There would be a plume of white smoke. There was a small tin hut above the beach west of Machair House, Ruaig, where the observers would shelter as they marked the accuracy of the bombing runs. Then the planes would sweep over Soay, turn again and come in. We would sit on the dunes and watch. Once, the planes let off a round of machine gun fire at the rocks. The horses in Alasdair Point's croft went wild with the noise.'*
Duncan Grant, Ruaig.

Squadron duties in Coastal Command we lost 69 crew members, with the loss of 19 aircraft. Two German U-boats were destroyed and we partially damaged many others, with unknown results.'

Despite this rightly proud record, Rex Watson wrote to say 'I was really surprised to hear that you are interested in 304 Polish Squadron. In my experience most historians treat the Polish subject with taboo. It started when Winston Churchill erased the name of General Sikorski from his memoirs.

'My rank was Corporal, (trade - Fitter 2A). In May 1942 we went to Tiree, where all our Wellingtons had to be resprayed white. We didn't mind being so far from "civilisation," as we had no families to go to, and sinking U-boats was as important as dropping bombs. For most of us it was another adventure.

'Most girls who worked in the NAAFI were local girls. They spoke Gaelic to each other, and our English wasn't all that good. But they never remarked that we talked in "gibberish," like their counterparts on the mainland. Once we organised a concert with local talents. The girls danced and sang in Gaelic. There was one piper who gave a magnificent performance. It was really an evening to remember.'

Mr Watson has one final comment. 'Without waterproof clothing I was wet all day long. There was practically no fuel for the stove, so everybody had to sleep fully clothed. In my opinion, every Nissen hut was connected with an underground passage, direct to the North Pole! But to compensate the bad points, I will add that fishing was very good and some nights it was so light that we could have a game of football at midnight.' Mr Watson changed his name after the war, to make it easier to obtain work.

304 Squadron published a wonderful record of their wartime service entitled 'Destiny Can Wait'. In the section on Tiree the following is recorded:

'When No. 304 (Polish) Bomber Squadron was transferred in May 1942 one of the senior Naval officers in Headquarters Coastal Command gruffly remarked, when he heard that the Squadron had been detailed off to Western Approaches: "They won't do it, they're too nervous." But the transition from the Battle of Germany to the Battle of the Atlantic proved surprisingly swift and smooth. The Polish crews found the sea less menacing on closer acquaintance, and even, after a few months, got to like it. Their new aerodrome was on the tiny Isle of Tiree in the Western Isles, washed by the Atlantic and swept by powerful winds as changeable and capricious as the weather. There were no navigational aids, or next to none, on the long anti-submarine patrols carried out by crews who had never seen a submarine.

'The Squadron needed a mascot. Every self-respecting unit should have a mascot. The local goats were Scottish Nationalists however, and refused every advance. The under-sized cows were specially protected by the Department of Agriculture for Scotland, and were sacrosanct. There were of course the seagulls – thousands of them. But who ever heard of a tame seagull? There were few dogs on the island. Dogs are sensible creatures.

'224 and 304 Squadrons got to know each other at a grand party. There was rivalry but friendly rivalry – who would sink the first U-boat? When one of 304's crews ditched in the Atlantic the OC of 224 Squadron had all his crews ready within half-an-hour to fly in search.'

Flying Officer F. Krzyszczuk, a navigator, wrote about an operational flight in the Squadron diary. 'It was still dark when we were awakened. We got up in the regulation way – immediately! We took off and were already heading across the ocean before daybreak. Nothing happened for a long time. We must have made about 300 miles. Leiba, the co-pilot, had just polished off the remaining sandwiches and coffee and yelled "oil-spot to starboard!" I could clearly see a triangular patch in the waves. It was undoubtedly a U-boat. There was a white line of foam from the periscope and a hollow in the waves over the conning tower. The kite dived from 2,000 to 50 feet, in less than no time, straight for the U-boat. I let go a "stick" of all six depth charges, and they hit the sea in a line 30 feet long astride the triangle. "Some fountain!" exclaimed the tail gunner. The six plumes of water really looked grand. They went up to our height. Some said, after a few drinks, the water splashed their face!

'We circled over the spot. A patch of oil formed, followed by another, then another and yet another. Great bubbles of air were breaking on the surface. We kept circling and dropped a few sea markers. We were highly commended at base for our good work. The sea markers were particularly appreciated (by the Royal Navy). We were officially told that the U-boat would be counted as "probably slightly damaged". A sanguine people, the British!'

Fascinating study of airmen and Wellington Bomber, taken by a 304 (Polish) Squadron photographer at Tiree. (Captain Milewski and Mr Deluga, Sikorski Museum)

One remarkable event at Tiree was the arrival of the Polish Airforce Standard. This had been produced in secret by women and nuns in Wilno (now Vilnius, Lithuania), despite the fact that Russia had occupied that part of Poland. It became a symbol of the unity of Poles suffering occupation at home and airmen fighting for freedom overseas. The embroidery thread was obtained by neutral diplomats from of all places, Berlin! The Standard spent 3 months with each Polish squadron in Britain and was treated with reverence. It was in 304's care while they were on Tiree. The flag had a red Polish Knight's cross with Our Lady of Ostra Brama on one side (with the words 'God, Honour, Fatherland') and St Theresa on the other, one side (with 'Love Demands Sacrifice'). Incredibly, the flag was smuggled out of Poland by Japanese diplomats in 1940 (they had not entered the war by then). In the picture we see Wing Commander Poziomek of 304 hand the Standard over to the CO of 305 Squadron. Poziomek was later killed when his aircraft was shot down in 1944. (Sikorski Museum)

'The leave-taking of Tiree was sadder than the squadron could have believed possible when they had first arrived at the lonely island, under the benevolent leadership of Group Captain Tuttle. It was he who arranged for the Coastal Command band to come all the way from England to play the Squadron on its way when it left Tiree on 13 June 1942. He took leave of every airman in person, and wished No. 304 Squadron "Good luck and good hunting".'

It would be good to leave this section with a happy ending. However, Polish ex-combatants recall that in 1946 the British government was so concerned with the possibility of offending Stalin's Soviet Russia that the Poles were our only Allies not invited to take part in the first anniversary VE parade in London. Some groups, including trade unionists, suggested that Polish ex-servicemen be encouraged to return to their homeland, now behind the 'Iron Curtain'. Most of those who did return to Poland at this point were imprisoned or 'disappeared'.

# CHAPTER 6

## Flotsam and Wet Some

Tiree's shores in wartime bore witness to the astonishing power of stormy seas as well as the tumultuous happenings just beyond view.

'Long before they started sending personnel in here, the driftwood was coming ashore, and other timber too for building or whatever. I remember one evening going down to the shore, maybe about 1941. By this time I was working for a farmer down the road, they were MacNivens, and I went down to the shore for a walk. Do you know this, I'm not exaggerating now, I could have walked thirty paces out onto the ocean, dry shod, on timber. Yes, I've never seen anything like it. Worth thousands and thousands of pounds, and young and all, and silly as I was, I thought, what in the name of God is this all about, this waste! And that was not all of it – the lives that were lost too, you see. What was the idea of it all?

'There were two or three rafts came ashore. They were intended if survivors at sea, maybe for a spell of time, were in need of provisions. That's all some of the rafts held – provisions, chocolate. Candle wax came ashore and I was one of them that made a few candles out of it. Casks of turpentine; 40 or 50 gallons. Ether coming ashore in big casks. Survival rations couped [tipped] out of a lifeboat or something. There was a chap up here, I happened to be with him. We shared it between us – chocolates, tobacco. He was a pipe smoker and I was a cigarette smoker. We got our share.

'I remember the first body that came ashore on this shore of ours. It was near Christmas time, and a local chap, a brother he was of Captain Donald Sinclair, Archie, we went down fishing off the rocks there for saithe, and we noticed gulls wheeling round at sea. We didn't realise or think of anything in that line. Later on a body was washed ashore there. He was dressed in civilian clothes and it was established that he must have been Italian. He had a dress suit on, collar and tie, shoes. Well dressed and all. It was said at the time that he was either from the City of Benares, or the Blue Star liner the *Andorra Star*; taking Italians over to Canada, putting them in camps there since Italy had joined in the war. There were quite a few bodies washed ashore. The police and the doctor were always informed. They were buried in the cemetery. One or two of them were taken away. There was one, there, a young lad, he was buried in the cemetery, but shortly after the cessation of hostilities he was taken away. He was supposed to have been off a German submarine that was sunk out there. She was caught sowing mines by the Sunderlands that were stationed at Oban. His name, I don't know what you would make of his name, language ways I mean, *Fogievurlaub*, I remember it well.' Hugh MacLean, Barrapol.

'A lot of flotsam came ashore on Tiree during the war and some people became keen beach collectors. One man was so keen it was said he would go through the pockets of a corpse to see what he could find. One day a neighbour lay down by the water's edge on Crossapol beach, to trick him. Sure enough the man came along and stood by the body. "I don't know who you are but you have a good pair of boots." He

Two Tiree school teachers, Jean Harvey and Jean Duff, sitting on a Carley float which had washed ashore in Balephetrish Bay. The SS *Malve* is visible, grounded on rocks, in the background. (Dimond)

*'The tanker* Lariston *came ashore at Craignish, over 10,000 tons; herself and another one, over at the Green, the* Ingrid. *I wasn't near the* Ingrid. *She was stuck on a rock about half a mile out at sea. But I was aboard the* Lariston *with the rest of the boys there.'* Hugh MacLean.

started to unlace them but the neighbour gave him a good kick and the man ran off in fear of his life!' John George MacLean, Scarinish

Perhaps in reaction to the *Sturdy* grounding, the Admiralty posted Lieutenant Commander Erick Naslund (of Swedish descent) to Tiree. He commanded a small Royal Navy unit at Scarinish and brought his wife and two children, with another son born while at Tiree. Naslund assumed responsibility for shipping around the island. One responsibility was preventing looting from wrecks. However, having made good friends among the islanders, he was known for giving the local people a 'sporting chance' before he arrived at a 'wreck'.

Other authorities chose to react in a different way. 'The school was closed yesterday as it was used for a shipwrecked crew. The lost attendance will be made up by opening on Saturday'. Scarinish School Log, 10 February 1942.

George Holleyman was with the RAF at Kilkenneth. 'My two-and-a-half-year stay on Tiree coincided with the grimmest period of the Battle of the Atlantic, when a huge tonnage of Allied merchant shipping was lost – the victims of German submarine warfare. The rocky headlands and sandy bays of Tiree were strewn with flotsam and jetsom from this carnage. There were vast quantities of timber, bales of rubber and cotton, barrels of tallow, as well as ships' lifeboats, Carley floats, rafts and other naval and merchant marine miscellanea.

'Three steamships were wrecked on the island of Tiree in the winter of 1941–2, all in the month of January. One wet and very windy night I was just finishing my Guard Room duty at Kilkenneth and booking back into camp, technical personnel from the evening shifts at Barrapol and Ben Hough. Just before midnight a telephone message came through that a vessel was in difficulty close to the shore at Mannel. We were asked to collect two or three local volunteer coastguards and take them to the scene of the disaster.

'It was very dark, with strong gusts of wind and bouts of squally rain from the west. About one hundred yards from the water's edge, one could just discern the black hulk of the *Ocean Tide* lying at a dangerous angle, with waves and spray continuously breaking over her. As one's eyes got accustomed to the gloom the figures of the crew could be seen on the deck. The men we had brought joined the coastguard group and were attempting to operate a tri-pod-like apparatus for firing rockets attached to lines. These efforts were not meeting with much success. Waves came in and it had to be moved back. This happened several times and there seemed little chance of getting lines across.'

'Presently we were joined by the RAF officer in charge, Group Captain Tuttle. He had brought a portable searchlight, which was soon lighting up the stricken ship. The constantly buffeted vessel was beginning to list ever more dangerously. The crew on the ship were also making efforts to get lines ashore. At about 2.00 am Group Captain Tuttle stripped off his oilskins, tunic and hat and swam through the icy waters to a reef. He managed to detach one of the lines. He then returned to the shore, but when he pulled on the cord we found, alas, that it had parted from the rope.

'By about 3.00 am the *Ocean Tide* was keeling over so badly it seemed liable to overturn. Suddenly there was a shout as the searchlight showed a small boat being launched. The seamen were making a last desperate throw and to the onlookers it seemed almost an act of madness. Six men could be seen straining feverishly with the oars to turn the boat so that the stern would be at right angles to the pounding waves. Within a few minutes it became apparent that they had lost control and the frail craft was being driven broadside towards the rocks.

'A number of us ran and clambered along the rocks to where the boat would strike. I reached the end with Group Captain Tuttle, to find that the furthest rocks were separated from us by a channel of swirling water about ten feet wide. By a miraculous chance two of the ropes which had been fired from the land were stretched across this passage and when we pulled on them we found they were tightly fixed. A few minutes later the boat struck the headland and flying oars and six men were shot on to the tiny plateau of glistening black rocks. Again, as if some supernatural agency was helping them, all the men managed to gain a foothold or cling successfully without being washed away. We shouted and indicated the ropes and one-by-one they struggled across the channel. At times they were almost completely submerged, with just a head or a hand showing above the waves. Eventually the six men (one of them injured) were dragged from the water and passed back over the rocks to safety.

'I later saw these men, safe, dry and partially recovered in the cookhouse of the Reef RAF Station. They looked a very tough, hard-bitten, but thankful group. The *Ocean Tide* was a fishing trawler from Leith.'

John Creal was a merchant seaman who experienced first-hand the difficulties of the unforgiving Atlantic storms. 'I was serving on an oil-tanker SS *Laristan* bound for America, for a cargo of oil. We formed convoy in Loch Ewe and came down the Isles in a tremendous storm with visibility almost nil. We were informed, whilst off Tiree, that the Commodore's ship had altered course to due west. Us, and I think three other vessels, altered course accordingly in blind faith, assuming that we must be clear of the island (we were not!). The other vessels collided with the rocks off-shore and were eventually floated off. We being in ballast, and so of lesser draught, piled right up on the shore in the dark of night.

'We spent two nights being pounded on the rocks, and were taken off by breeches-buoy. Our first night ashore was spent with the RAF lads of the DF station, with whom we shared a large jar of rum (also rescued by breeches-buoy). Accommodation was found for us with the islanders. I and some others stayed with some sisters named MacKinnon.'

Alice Atkins had moved to Tiree to be with her husband and her stay coincided with this eventful period. 'On 19 January 1942 after a stormy day or two, a convoy of ships bound for South America was scattered around nearby islands, seeking shelter. One, the SS *Lariston* ran onto a rocky promontory behind the Hough. At the time my husband Bill was serving with the Royal Air Force on the Isle of Tiree, working on mobile radar vans, while awaiting the construction and erection of the radar masts on top of the Hough.

'Our own home at that time was on the south coast of England, which was not very safe due to the threat of German invasion, hence my presence on Tiree with our young son. We stayed with the Cameron family at Balevullin, a lovely caring and helpful family; Murdoch, Peggy and their three sons, Donald, Lachie and Allan. Murdoch was the Chief Coastguard who performed "watches" at the "look-out" hut behind the shoulder of the Hough, along with other locals. Fine men they were too.

'Murdoch, I believe, was on duty at the "look-out" on a Wednesday night when the *Lariston* was driven onto the rocks. The Captain refused assistance to take the crew off, because he was hopeful of floating his vessel off the rocks at high tide. This he attempted to do over the space of at least two further high tides, without success.

The SS *Lariston*, on the rocks at Craignish point. She was later salvaged. The *Lariston* belonged to the Hindustan Oil Co., of Newcastle.

*'The* Lariston *lay some 2 miles from a road, so initially the salvage process and supplies had to be accessed from the sea. In June 1942 a steel gangway of more than 400ft was erected. When the sea engulfed the wreck supplies had to be dropped onto the deck by planes flying from the Reef'.* (Holleyman)

'On the Friday following, I was walking in the gathering darkness towards the Cameron croft, from the shop in Balevullin kept by Mistress Cameron. Suddenly the sky above the Hough erupted with the sight and sound of "maroons" which gave a fright. The safety and condition of the *Lariston* had deteriorated and the captain had decided it was time to abandon ship.

'The men of Tiree answered the call and took part in the rescue of the *Lariston* crew. All gave of their best and more. It was pitch-black and what with the lack of proper roads and atrocious weather, progress was extremely slow. The weather worsened considerably, the seas became mountainous and the wind gusted to hurricane force. God help all men who sail the seas, especially in times of war. Tiree people know this only too well. They reached the area and set up their equipment in preparation for firing a line over the bows of the *Lariston*. Apparently the first few firings were unsuccessful due predominantly to the hurricane force winds and lack of adequate lighting. Eventually as the day dawned a line was secured and the rescue began.

'Peggy prepared food and hot drinks for Allan and myself to take round in baskets. We set off loaded and suitably clad against the weather for our long walk. Allan seemed to know instinctively that the best route was to round the Hough at the Sandaig end, but it was not at all easy and we had great difficulty standing upright; the wind buffeted and pulled at us constantly. With the rocky terrain and uneven ground I was unable to keep my footing and twice I fell, but amazingly managed to retrieve the bags of provision.

'We eventually arrived to a chilling scene – the mountainous seas screaming and crashing violently and incessantly over the vessel, lying helplessly at the end of the promontory of jagged rocks. The wind was a tempestuous, howling enemy but a trial run with a keg of rum ensured that the breeches-buoy was in fact secure.

'Murdoch was shouting instructions in Gaelic to his team of rescuers but many of the words were dispersed in the wind and the beating, sheeting rain. He frequently passed messages to Bill in English for him to send by Aldis lamp to those on board.

'As Allan and I got closer we were unable to recognise anyone because the salt from the spray had encrusted their faces. Then the first seaman was secured in the breeches-buoy. Murdoch's team, up to 10 of them, began heaving on the ropes. Several times the men went under the mountainous sea, then onto the rocks until finally being hauled safely to land. It was horrific. The screeching, moaning wind and the incessant noise and in the midst of all that, those gallant men heaving away, every inch gained a heroic effort. Even with the 10 men hauling with all their strength, each rescue took at least 15 to 20 long, long minutes to achieve. Salty wet ropes do not run smoothly.

'The team remained throughout that day and well into the next, fighting against the odds in the most awful conditions imaginable, absolutely exhausted, until the task was complete. All forty mariners, and a wee terrier dog with the last man, were saved – all in reasonable shape. The crew were all taken to John Brown's hotel at Scarinish in order to recover from their ordeal, before reaching Oban where they were dispersed.

'I wonder how many of that crew, if any, and how many more men of the Merchant Navy survived the war; a terrible time I wish to forget.'

It is recorded in the annals of British merchant shipping [the much under-acknowledged '4th arm' of the services in WW2] that the violent storms of January 1942 were of such severity they caused more than 20 vessels to be pitched, hurled or tossed onto the shores of west Scotland, the islands or Northern Ireland. The tanker *Lariston* was 'lifted' by the mountainous seas and crashed ashore on Craignish Point. So grave was her predicament that it is said the underwriters 'paid-up' almost immediately, declaring her 'a total loss'. A salvage ship wisely decided not to approach the ragged, rocky outcrops until the venomous conditions abated. In the first 21 days after the grounding, the salvage officer only dared venture on board the *Lariston* for a total of 2 hours, before returning to safety. However, word came from the Admiralty in London, she had to be salvaged. Tankers were indispensable to the 'war effort'.

Remarkable ingenuity was deployed to blow away rocks, above and below the sea and divers bolted on temporary plates below the surface. Her tanks were cleared of sea water and the *Lariston* was eventually manoeuvred seaward at a precarious angle. By the end of July she was able to make her way to the Clyde, supported by tugs. After repairs she sailed again as the *Empire Gulf*.

Iain Clark writes evocatively of how he viewed the war, as a schoolboy visiting Coll. 'On 29 July 1942 I was eight years of age, enjoying our annual holiday on the island of Coll, staying with my mother and father in the home of Colin and Mary Mackinnon in their thatched cottage at Bousd.

'My mother and I would go for the duration of the school holidays and my father would join us for his fortnight's annual leave. We went not only with all our luggage, but with all the food and treats that my mother had been collecting and stockpiling through the darkest days of rationing, to take to her aunt and uncle, to supplement what they would willingly provide from their slender resources.

'The sun shone on long lovely days, on deserted white strands and on trips to the peat moss with grand-uncle Colin, to restack the drying peats. If he was in the right mood, and I had behaved myself, I was given the opportunity to drive and guide the horse.

'Towards evening this day we were returning to Bousd. My father and I were walking in front as an ever-thickening mist was rolling in from the Atlantic. As it spread and intensified the temperature dropped and visibility gradually lessened. From a distance a ship's siren came, muffled through the mist. Eerily, through the grey fluffiness of the mist, it sounded at regular intervals. My father stood still and motioned by hand that I do likewise.

'"He's in danger, in real trouble!" With that he launched himself off the road and across the machair towards the shore. Then there was the exhilaration of running at breakneck speed across the coarse grass, over rocky outcrops, through some marshy patches, until we came close to the shore. All this time the sound of the siren came ever closer.

'We crossed the last ridge of rock to see the *Nevada 11* still, at rest, some fifty feet from the shore: a large grey ship with engines running and steam issuing from funnel and other points. It was as if she had come in to tie up alongside these rocks. I remember the surging water at the stern of the ship, as engines were put in reverse to try to move the vessel from the rocks on which she was stuck fast. I could see men at the bow and stern of the ship and hear shouts from them, to the men on the bridge, but I could not understand because they spoke a foreign language. They must be German!

'My father informed me they were French and started to make verbal contact. He was a native Hebridean, an officer in the Northern Lighthouse Service, with an encyclopaedic knowledge of the coast. It seems the ship's navigators had been listening for a fog horn, which had been silenced for war-time purposes.

'It was by a considerable margin the largest ship I had seen at 5,693 tons. Every part of her deck was crowded with huge army trucks of all shapes and sizes and a number of magnificent naval launches, shining, highly polished, fast-looking craft with streamlined cabins.

'Other people began to arrive, the news spreading as it does on an island which did not have a single telephone in the East End, as the Sorisdale, Bousd, Cornaig area was known. An RAF signal post had been established on the island and I remember a man in uniform being among the first to arrive. I did not want to go home, as I examined every inch of the ship as darkness gradually deepened and the mist settled lower and thicker. I was glad for the comfort of my father's hand as we walked carefully back to the house to end the most adventurous day of my life.

'Auntie Mary and Uncle Colin were brother and sister, both probably in their seventies. I see Mary forever in a wrap round print apron with thick black stockings and sandshoes, her white hair drawn back into a bun from a ruddy, lined face which could break into a welcoming smile, particularly for loved ones and children. At other times her expression was stern and her manner shy and retiring. She had never been off the island. They may once have kept sheep or cattle with some other farm stock but the only thing they had around the house then were hens. I helped Colin with them. They were truly free range, having the run of the island, after they were let out of the henhouse in the morning and before they were rounded up in the gloaming. There were perhaps 15–18 hens and Colin knew each one by name. At nightfall the task was finding the straggler. Having counted them all in, in Gaelic: *un, dhea, tra, quarer.*

'This day, looking for the eggs had turned from a pleasure to a chore, until at last Colin, my mother and father were all set to take me to the *Rhu Mhor* rocks where the *Nevada* lay. When we arrived the vantage points above the vessel were dotted with locals and visitors who had come from all over the island to see the sight. A tug arrived, standing some mile away, beyond the reefs. My father read the Morse messages being flashed by Aldis lamp from the tug. The tug was not authorised to do anything until the surveyors had made their examination. They were en-route from London, as I remember, but would be off the next mail boat on Wednesday. I was so proud of my father's expertise and knowledge. I resolved there and then to stick in at my signalling at the Cubs.

'The *Nevada* had launched a lifeboat on the starboard side and members of the crew had come ashore to mingle with the onlookers. They were mostly of West African origin, in their working clothes, with very limited English, but offering "Duty Free" cigarettes as a show of their willingness to be friendly. Later stories were told of some of them reaching the hotel and being mildly wild on a few pints of its finest, but that is what the stories would say.

'The great Atlantic rollers broke all over the *Nevada* in her uneasy resting place and by the time we visited next morning her stern had dipped into the waves and her back was broken. By the time the surveyors arrived on the *Lochearn*, even an eight-year-old could tell that the stricken ship would never be moved from the rocks on which she lay.

'The *Nevada's* crew packed their belongings and left for Oban on the mail boat. A naval party arrived as the weather improved and placed all the shining launches in the water and spirited them off to the naval base in Tobermory. Within a week we too had packed our bags and returned to Oban, to restart at Rockfield School, with a tale or two to tell in the playground, but only to tried and trusted friends, as we knew that "walls had ears".

'Next year we returned to Coll for the summer holiday. Relatives had visited in the meantime and I had heard the name *Nevada* occurring in various Gaelic conversations, but any enquiries on my part had been met with bland statements about salvage work. We arrived in the early afternoon and went to Auntie Katie's in the middle of the street in Arinagour, for a meal before getting a car to the East End.

'A friend from previous years of my own age, who had been evacuated from Glasgow for the duration of the war, came to call. We walked along the main street, which was lined with lorries of the type I had seen on the decks of the *Nevada* the year before. "Can you go on them?" I asked Neil. "Of course, I'll take you to the one I call mine. All the boys at school have one of their own." He led me to a real monster bristling with bars and brackets and places where equipment seemed to have been removed. He sat in the driver's seat and made all the appropriate noises as he went through the gears. After a while he graciously moved over and allowed me to have my turn. What a start to the holiday!

'"Come and have a look in here, this is our den." Neil announced, as he pulled from his pocket a box of matches and lit a candle, pulled out a tin and proffered it towards me.

"Do you want a smoke?" It was a flat, fifty tin of State Express 333 cigarettes. "No thanks, I don't smoke" I stammered out. "Everyone on Coll does, even *Mhari Mhor*, and she's over ninety and didn't start until after the *Nevada*." He pulled on his cigarette and started to tell me that the ship was found to be carrying a very mixed cargo, including NAAFI stores, intended for troops in West Africa. The salvors sometimes kept a crate "for themselves". They would take a few tins home to friends and neighbours, who would then get together at night and visit the ship to get some more "for themselves". All the cigarettes were packed in tins, either flat fifties like the State Express, or in round, water-tight tins. Coll's shop had stopped asking for its tobacco allocation, as there was no sale.

'Salvage workers were recruited. A monkey bridge [of ropes and wood] was constructed between the rocks and the stricken ship, to give easier access to the workers by day and of course, to raiding parties by night. The alternative route was by small boat, which was used by those from Tiree and perhaps further afield, who were known to have visited. The morality of the raids aboard *Nevada* is interesting. No one had lured this ship onto the *Rhu Mhor* rocks in Struan Bay. This was a "bounty" sent to Coll in dark days, as surely as The Lord sent occasional good harvests. Goods cast upon the shore and put to use on the island would be a universal truth from people living on a coastline anywhere in the world. Men of impeccable honesty, who would never covet their neighbour's ox or ass would take from the ship what they needed rather than see it line the pockets of a southern entrepreneur.

'*Nevada* crockery and cutlery turned up in the most unlikely places, as did the famous print. In the cargo were bales of printed cotton in rather garish colours and designs, not generally seen in British shops or catalogues. However in times of rationing when clothing coupons were required, the cloth was soon in service throughout the island as curtains, chair covers and bedspreads. One day some Customs officials made their way to Coll on the *Lochearn*. But in the way of these things, their destinations and the possible purpose of the visit was established before the ship made her call at Tobermory, from where a telephone call could be made to alert the population of the island.

'Some of the material found its way further afield and there is a lovely story of someone looking for a family with a Coll connection who lived on Dumbarton Road, Glasgow. Unfortunately the address had been mislaid and as Dumbarton Road runs to over 2,000 numbers, it seemed a lost cause. However, the would-be visitor was made of sterner stuff and he persevered, walking along the road examining the tenement windows, until he came to one with *Nevada* print curtains! Shoes discovered by a raiding party turned out to be all for the right foot, as they are generally so packed to combat theft. It was said that one rather mean islander hobbled around with toes of his shoes packed with rolled up newspapers rather than admit defeat.

'On one summer night expedition, piles of brand new West African 20 shilling notes were discovered. This would no longer be compared to "taking one for the pot". This would be crime. A merchant navy man used his considerable authority to instruct them to take no part of it, not even a souvenir note. That night no one did. However notes were found on the beach at Cornaig not far from the *Nevada's* resting place. Some were offered to a Scottish bank and some were handed to the local Receiver of Wrecks.

'The final bonanza was the coal from the ships fuel bunkers, which delayed peat cutting on the island for at least one season. Eventually much of the ship was cut down for scrap metal and the salvors departed. That was the end. Well almost. In February 1960, almost eighteen years after the *Nevada* grounded, one of the salvors walked into the offices of a currency dealer in Zurich and exchanged 19,749 West African 20 shilling notes for 200,000 Swiss francs. In a three-day trial, in November 1962 at the High Court in Edinburgh, the salvor was sentenced to nine months imprisonment. And the remaining notes unaccounted for? Does there still exist a hand-drawn map, indicating a treasure trove worth digging for, beneath a lonely strand on Coll?'

# CHAPTER 7

## Radar and Ground Crew

Tiree was selected to host radar installations during the Second World War. At the time this was absolutely top secret technology. 'Hush, Hush' and 'Huff Duff' [high frequency direction finding] were mentioned in muted tones. But the vast majority did not talk at all about such matters. The servicemen who made this technology 'work', and those who staffed the numerous 'unglamorous' ground trades, have received precious little acclamation throughout the years – let us try to redress the balance a little here.

David Withers was one of the young 'pioneers'. 'Around September 1942 I had finished my basic training as a ground radar mechanic and I was posted to Port Mòr. Down in the south, Tiree was not well-known, and the name has a rather glamorous ring to it. Minds tend to fly to dusky maidens by South Pacific seas. I still remember the few months I was there with pleasure, although dusky maidens did not feature in it, nor for that matter did undusky ones!

'On the old *Hebrides* we did not have a comfortable journey – a longish day, with not many bits of deck gear around that were sufficiently free of oil and water to be sat on. At twenty I was an unsociable youngster. We had bicycles available to get from one of the radar sites to another when motor transport was not available. I regret I made pitifully little effort to get to know the island outside the immediate neighbourhood of Kilkenneth. This site was made up of 20 to 30 Nissen huts which provided living accommodation for about 150 men. There was also an Orderly Room, Officers' Mess, stores and motor transport sheds. A couple of young ladies, probably from Balevullin, staffed the NAAFI canteen. A lot of the servicemen were Scots, although a considerable number were English and there was a handful of Australians. This base camp provided living quarters for the crews of three radar stations which were called Port Mòr, Ben Hough and Barrapol. There was a fourth radar site between Ben Hough and the sea, confusingly called Kilkenneth.

A Halifax of 518 Squadron Tiree, taking off over Ben Hough, showing Radar masts at RAF Kilkenneth (below aircraft nose). Also visible is the site of the RAF accommodation at Kilkenneth/Hough (to rear of aircraft tail) and Balevullin township and beach. The Met Observer can be seen in the perspex nose of the Halifax. (Campbell)

'When I think back to Tiree, I remember not people, but green hillocks unspoilt by the mass of humanity, blue skies containing small rain clouds being blown in from the sea and ditches full of irises. There was a general store at Balevullin and occasionally I walked across the dunes to buy some odd thing there – some razor blades maybe. I usually found the shopkeeper chatting to a customer in Gaelic. As far as I could see all the islanders but the quite old spoke excellent English.

'I had developed a strong interest in radio and electronics. In the mid-1930s several of the bigger industrial nations were conscious of the need to have the means available for detecting aircraft at a sufficiently early stage in an air raid. They were all seeking solutions based on transmitting a powerful radio signal from a ground station, listening for an echo reflected by an aircraft, then locating a source of that echo. The UK knew that it was in peril. Hardware [already developed for television broadcasting] was put together. This British system was called 'Chain Home' (CH) and was excellent at detecting single high-flying aircraft at long distance. Next was the Auxiliary Chain Home (ACH) system, a version that could be moved around and set up in a few days, using sectionalised wooden masts about 70 feet high. Then in 1940–1, came a system that could detect low flying aircraft much more effectively than CH. This provided protection against low flying aircraft and was called Chain Home Low (CHL).

'When war broke out our enemy was to the east. As far as I know, no radar stations were installed on the west coast in the first year or so of the war. But Germany overran Norway in April and France by June 1940. The situation was transformed and action was taken to build up radar defences down the west coast and, no doubt, to protect as well may be, the sea lanes into Glasgow, Liverpool and the "Western Approaches".

'When I arrived, the CHL stations on Ben Hough and at Barrapol, and the ACH station at Port Mòr, had clearly been in business for a year or so. The three stations would have complemented one another – Ben Hough and Barrapol covering jointly most of the sea area to the north of Ireland and meshing in with other posts on Barra and Benbecula. Port Mòr was providing additional protection from lone raiders that might slip by the CHL stations. All three reported their sightings to a Filter Room at The Reef where they sorted the "wheat from the chaff" and passed the wheat to a Fighter Operations Room. A new version of the CH system, using transmitters designed for ACH but with high antenna masts, was then introduced and installed along the west coast. Kilkenneth was one of these sites.

'My posting was to Port Mòr and I worked there for three or four months. Then I and the rest of the Port Mòr crew were transferred to Kilkenneth. It was technically a very good site for the purpose, on dunes which sloped down for a few hundred yards to the sea. Then the station was taken out of operation, being put on a "care-and-maintenance" basis. I was one of a handful of radar mechanics that was to keep it in comfortable idleness until a pressing need for it should arise. The rest of the old Port Mòr hands were posted away from Tiree and the ACH equipment likewise.'

Jack Liddy was also posted to RAF Kilkenneth. 'There was one domestic site where the RAF was billeted on that side of the island at the foot of Ben Hough. When I first arrived, there were no proper toilets, baths or showers. If you wanted a bath you had to have it in a tin bath, in the billet, in front of about 20 other airmen.

RAF men at Kilkenneth Camp, with their mascot. (Parker)

'Living conditions at Kilkenneth were a bit spartan for town lads, even then. We were sleeping about twenty to a Nissen. The sleeping huts were not in particularly good condition; very draughty and with a tendency for water to creep in under the doors. However, the roofs didn't leak too much. There was a small but powerful coke stove in each hut. We had no piped hot water, but each hut had one cold water tap. Lavatories were of the bucket variety.'
David Withers.

'There were four radar operators and one mechanic on each watch. The worst part of the job was walking up and down Ben Hough, sometimes twice a day. I spent most of my time up on Ben Hough, which was still operational when I left Tiree. It had a revolving aerial which went practically 360 degrees and then reversed. If the wind was too strong the aerials had to be stopped and lashed down. This meant climbing the aerials to fix the cables – a very hazardous job!

'The NAAFI was the centre of the entertainment. There was a very good five-piece band at the "drome" and they used to visit us once a week. They had a vocalist called Freddie Holmes who in private life was lead singer with the "Radio Revellers", very popular before and after the war. I became their regular drummer. We also had one or two musicians amongst our radar staff on the camp and ran our own band for dances, which the islanders used to attend. One of the locals used to bring his bagpipes. Nigel Hill was a professional base fiddle player and was with Jack Payne's band immediately prior to being called up. I remember one Christmas at a NAAFI concert we gave a rendering of "Big Noise from Winnetka", a speciality number for bass fiddle and drums.'

Freddie Holmes, a musician who was stationed at RAF Kilkenneth, with his band. Freddie was something of a star in civilian life with the 'Radio Revellers' band. (Holmes)

Hough NAAFI. (An Iodhlann)

*'Folk like myself didn't travel far very often in those days, not even to the Reef. Hut K1 was the bar in Kilkenneth. Donald Cameron would keep an eye out for the lorry bringing supplies from the Reef. He would then get word to Archie MacLean and others – "It's a small barrel today, be early!" Sometimes, in winter, they would put a poker in the beer to warm it up'.* Donald MacKinnon, Hough.

Jim Fowler remembers, 'The Ben Hough camp was made up of different trades connected with radar – radar operators, radar mechanics, diesel engineers, motor transport drivers and mechanics, a few general duty people, cooks and 3 or 4 officers, mostly for administration. Much of the time spent at Ben Hough was either "on watch" in the radar block at the top of the hill, or in bed, because for much of the time there we were on a 3-watch system, with little time off.

'We were all issued with black, heavy waterproof macs and sou'westers because in winter the rain came at you horizontally. It was quite a climb up winding steps to the brow of the hill. The radar block itself, housed the transmitter and receiver and next to this building, on a large concrete structure, was the aerial. This could detect every aircraft within a range of over 100 miles. Inside the radar block, as well as the transmitter, there were two screens like TV receivers, one called a Plan Position Indicator (PPI) tube and a range finder. At Ben Hough we would normally have about a dozen aircraft on the screen at the one time. We would give the position of an aircraft by land-line to the Filter Room which was in Inverness. The Filter Room would almost immediately identify it as either hostile or friendly.

'We did have the occasional film show, once every three months perhaps, to which the "locals" were invited. They occupied the first three rows in the NAAFI. Most of the fair sex had the Christian name of Flora, it seemed! There was quite a good pitch about a mile away and the football matches were usually between Scots and English at the camp. On return to civvie-street I was "spotted" and eventually signed as an amateur for Leeds United.

'After a while I managed to find a wee place, not really big enough to be a cottage – a croft I suppose; one room, with a few chickens sharing the place with an elderly lady, who would supply us with eggs occasionally. She also, once or twice, did my washing. No ironing of course, as she didn't have electricity. The washing was done perfectly, in a pot on her peat fire, in return for a few coppers. That was all we could afford anyway, as I think my pay then was 3 shillings a day.'

Frank Hamp has fairly 'distinctive' memories of the island's north shore. 'Ben Hough is where I was destined. I had to endure the rigours of several weeks of concentrated military training. The assault course, a daily penance in between spells in the classroom, learning about guns. It possessed one diabolical feature, which would have brought tears to the eyes of even the toughest commando. The most feared obstacle on our assault course was a primitive, open cesspit, which we had to leap across in the full battle kit. One morning a Canadian airman fell into it and had to be flown straight to hospital, though physical injury he had none.'

One man who was ground crew on Tiree is keen to comment on the living conditions. Arnold Keeling recalls 'Washing of clothes was a nightmare on Tiree. At our living site we had a stream by our hut, from which we took water and heated it on the stove. Into this we put our dirty clothes then rinsed them in the stream. There used to be discussions on whether the stream water was brown due to the heather or the cows further up the field!'

George Hambling also thoroughly enjoyed Tiree and returned a number of times. 'My job in the RAF was in the signals section of Fighter Command. I trained as a Radio Telephony Operator/Direction Finding, with emphasis on VHF direction finding. I was one of the first batch of lads so trained at Cranwell. As a very ordinary LAC I was posted to Tiree in 1942 and I was there for about 12 months. It sounded like a long way from home and I was not thrilled about going there. I was told it was a bleak, windy place. The wind so strong you could just about lean back on it and not fall over!

'On Tiree we were attached to Coastal Command. I was stationed near Heanish, where I and two other Direction Finding Operators lived in a block hut and got our meals with Mrs MacDonald and Mrs MacKinnon. Mr "Mac" was the lighthouse keeper. He was a great fisherman too, away in his dinghy at crack of dawn, back with fish for breakfast. Best fish I've ever had.

'We operated a DF tower adjacent to our hut. The concrete floor of the hut is still there. At Heanish we were somewhat "out of sight, out of mind" of the main camps. We three operated a 24-hour watch system – always on duty. We did our job and looked after ourselves, doing our own washing and ironing. We had a stove in our hut for hot water and a chemical toilet that had to be emptied into a very big hole that we dug. All rather primitive really, but we were young and keen. At that time there were a few WAAFS working at our HQ, in Baugh. We saw them on the bus, but otherwise they were very much segregated, own compound etc, strictly out of bounds.

'In those days you kept the details of what job you were doing, and why, to yourself. Right from the start you were told not to talk about service matters, not to anyone. One event I clearly remember whilst at this site was that one afternoon our signals officer, Fl. Lt Guthrie, called on us and asked who was on duty next day, morning watch. I said I was. He said "Be on your toes as we are expecting a VIP". He did not say what or who. I thought it might be Winston C or someone high up. Things were very "hush hush".

'I was keeping a very sharp ear out for any sort of sound on the air, when suddenly an American voice, very, very loud came through "Hello Straw hat, are you receiving me?" (Straw hat was our call sign.) I snapped a bearing on him. He replied "That's Okay guy, I can see you, out". I took off my headphones and looked out a window, in time to see a Flying Fortress fly right over and then touchdown. The story went around that he had flown direct from Newfoundland and was one of the first to come over direct. Previously the planes had come on ships but too many were lost that way to U-boats.

'Whilst operating at this particular site we often had an elderly crofter drive by in a farm type cart, big wheels and big horse. He was a large man with a bushy moustache. He would be sitting hunched up on the front of the cart, old cap and old overcoat, pipe in mouth. We tried to speak to him on many occasions but didn't get much response. One day he stopped and asked about tobacco – he was obviously finding it hard to get it. We gave him a fill or two. After that he would speak as he passed by and one day brought us some fish. We asked about eggs and he invited us to his cottage to get some. From then on he supplied us with eggs in exchange for tobacco – the "heaviest" stuff we could get.'

'There was a little hut behind *Taigh a' Chiobair* [the Shepherd's House, now demolished] on the Reef. Two bunks and a bogey stove in the middle. There were two guys in there, Harry Skinner, from Kent, and Owen Ball. They used to talk the planes in, in bad weather or if an engine was down. They had a dog called 'Tiger'. He ate like a lord, better than we did. They used to fry sausages for 'Tiger' and make mashed potatoes. When they were on duty, they used to take me over with them and they used to say, "Don't tell anyone you were here." You weren't supposed to go in these places. My mother used to make scones for them. And they used to put a set of earphones on me and plug it into one of these sets and I could hear everything.' Hugh MacKinnon, Baugh.

Peter Whitworth was posted to the neighbouring island of Coll with the RAF. 'In 1942 I was on a wireless unit which covered the Western Isles. We were small wireless units plotting aircraft 24 hours a day. The HQ for our unit was a few Nissen huts at the rear of the harbour in Oban. There was a post on most islands, with a staff of around six personnel and one Austin van. I was on the Isle of Coll, about two miles from Arinagour, on the road to Sorisdale. I think it used to be a shooting lodge before the war. Other islands had our units including Tiree, Iona, Colonsay, Skye, Mull and also Ardnamurchan. Some of the lads with me were later killed in the Normandy landings. Our look-out post was made of logs with a corrugated iron roof, covered with turf with large radio aerials. This was built near a cliff, with the help of some islanders. We had a telephone cable from the post down to a house which was quite a long way down the hill.

'German aircraft were plotted as "unidentified". We took approximate height, distance and direction. We plotted quite a few Allied aircraft coming back damaged, some with engines out of action. We could hear Tiree and Iona pick up the plot after we had sent ours. We could view Eigg, Muck and Rum, with the Isle of Skye in the distance, on a clear day. We could see Iona with binoculars just about, but there wasn't many clear days.

'We used to get seamen who had been drowned washed up on Coll. We were the only military on the island of Coll and when someone reported bodies on the beach we had to go with the Austin van and take them to Arinagour. Sometimes they had been in the water for so long they were so heavy to lift it took four of us. There was a rumour that the *Queen Mary* had rammed a destroyer (HMS *Curacao*) and caused many casualties.

'We didn't get much sleep at nights when it was misty. They used to have a gun which fired on a time switch, with it being such dangerous waters. We used to wait at the Arinagour jetty twice a week for paraffin for the Tilley lamps and Valor stoves, petrol for the van, food rations and mail. MacBraynes did a good job during the war years but the *Hebrides* was too old when I was on it in 1942. We had to get down into the boats with the cattle when landing at Coll. The farmers on Coll looked after us very well. They gave us eggs and butter and vegetables.'

Kenneth Waller worked in the sick quarters on Tiree. 'It was away from the main airfield and camp [at Crossapol] and consisted of large Nissens linked by a central corridor. There were wards for WAAF and RAF personnel, an operating theatre, consulting rooms, dental surgery, offices and a kitchen (presided over by an Italian POW cook). Dr Hunter, the island GP, became involved at the end of the RAF's presence on Tiree.

'I have a fond memory of a crofter [Colin MacPhail] who also arranged bookings for islanders on the then Scottish Airways, who flew to the mainland. A Gaelic speaker, to my ear his English was the most beautiful I had then heard spoken.'

Molly Goold's contact with Tiree in wartime was by letter. 'My husband, Francis Goold, was in the RAF during the war. One of his last postings was to the island of Tiree. He wrote that if the weather was very bad the essential supplies of food, and in the early days even bread, did not get through. They were often hungry.

'Washing facilities at the camp were minimal and Francis used to post his laundry home to me. How I hated those stiff RAF shirts. When I returned the clean laundry I would try to include some little luxury such as a bar of chocolate, a tin of sardines, a packet of biscuits, none of which was easy to come by. I felt his need was greater than ours (myself and my two infant sons).

RAF Sick Bay personnel, Tiree, 1945. Front row right, in white shirt, is an Italian POW Orderly. (Waller)

'Francis was on the office staff and one of his tasks was to censor letters. One day a letter arrived asking if I could send him a fine-tooth comb with my next laundry parcel. My heart sank. I trotted off to our local chemist, waiting until the shop was empty. I bought two and also asked him for a tin of Keating's Insect Powder. Back came a letter thanking me for the clean laundry and enclosures but "Why the Keating's?" Apparently the soil was sandy and because of the constant winds the only way of getting the sand out of the hair was with such a comb. I hurried to the chemist anxious to reassure him that things were not quite as bad as I had thought.

'Members of the air crew were sometimes killed on operational flights. There was great competition to be one of the accompanying parties, which escorted the bodies back to the mainland. Francis sometimes managed to snatch a few hours at home when in one of these parties. One of his jobs was to make out the travel passes for any airmen who were being posted elsewhere. When he did so he always included the words "Has permission to visit home", and made out the warrant accordingly. This, he used to say, might be their last chance to see their loved ones.

Groundcrew at Tiree with the Air Sea Rescue detachment. (Anderson)

*'A day after we arrived there was the first snow storm for about twenty years. Drifts on the road were up to 6 feet deep and the runways were about four feet under. We cleared the roads so that supplies could get through but our attempts at clearing the runway failed miserably.'* Ron Hall.

Sergeants' Mess staff, the Reef. (Harry Smith – front, second right, Denis Guest, front left).

*'I was "posted overseas" in 1943: Tiree! What a beautiful island; if only it was nearer the Equator! I worked in the kitchens and took part in many of the RAF plays and musicals. I can't forget a line from one song "I'm on my knees in the Hebrides, because it's raining on Tiree".'* Harry Smith.

Francis promised that one day he would take me to Tiree, which he had grown to love. But the day never came. He died in 1962. My elder son, John, took me on a holiday to Scotland a few years ago and we stayed in Oban in a hotel. We didn't have time to visit Tiree but we sailed round Mull on one of the MacBraynes steamers. John pointed out Tiree, low on the skyline. I am ninety-two now, and will never visit the Island, but I will never forget the time my husband spent there and the kindness of the people who, having little themselves, shared what they had with the "invaders".

# CHAPTER 8

# 'They were Sophisticated'

'Thinking back on it now, the main memory, apart from the flying, was meeting the friendly local people. It was wonderful the way they looked after us.' Maurice Foster, Royal Australian Air Force.

One aspect of life on Tiree in WW2 is the story of the meeting of two cultures; one Gaelic-speaking, horse-powered and with most of its young men away, out-numbered by a mostly young, adrenaline-fuelled and multi-national air force contingent. Many islanders have potent memories of this time.

At first some servicemen were billeted around the island in local homes. This proximity led to some close relationships, and for Duncan Grant his first encounter with the tragedy of war. 'During the war you had to take someone in whether you liked it or not if you had accommodation in the household. The elderly lady in this house in Ruaig had a man placed with her – a Mr King. One man I particularly remember – Clem Greenlaw, an Australian. Because most of the men in Ruaig were elderly, this young man stood out. He came round to our house quite often, full of vitality. When we were reluctant to clean our teeth, my aunt would say, "Clem! Tell the boys to clean their teeth!" As long as Clem said it we were happy with that. When the snow came Clem was running around in the snow throwing snowballs. This was great fun for us as boys. And then we heard that Clem was going away, and then, to our horror, my aunt said one day that Clem had been killed. This was the war. His brave young life – he certainly put sparkle into us as boys. He was so full of life, the sense of fun that he had.'

Pat Eiles came to live on Tiree with her husband who was with 518 Squadron. 'It was with a Miss Munn and her brother. She said she had never seen anyone with make up on, or smelt perfume, so she got a shock when she met me! It was a nice, quaint little croft, not far from the sea, with a tin roof. You could hear the rain on it. Miss Munn read the Bible a lot, more so when my husband was on "ops".'

Mrs Pat Eiles, from London, whose husband was a pilot with 518 Squadron. She came to live on Tiree during the war. (Eiles)

Peter Clark, second left, a Flight Engineer with 518 Squadron, at Tiree, with his fellow crew members ('Brylcreem Boys'!). (Clark)

*'The Halifax was fitted with special extra fuel tanks, with depth charges carried in the wing bomb bays. Two or four aircraft went out every day whatever the weather conditions. I well remember hearing the ice, which had formed on the propellers and engines, flying off and come crashing against the sides of our fuselage.' Peter Clark.*

'Rocky' Stone with island girl, at a store in Balephuil. Rocky was later lost on an operational flight with Max Bacon's crew, in January 1945. (Bryce)

One of the main venues islanders met service personnel were the regular dances.

'I would leave the house in Cornaig and start walking. You wouldn't be walking very long when an RAF truck would come along and you'd get a lift. It was great during the war. I came home one New Year. There were a lot of dances going on at that time. Oh God! The dances! The RAF would send a truck round all the places. Nobody walked. Mary and I went this night. John Crawford, her boss, and his brother-in-law were at the dance. They got us something to drink, was it sherry? We were a wee bit tipsy! I remember getting up and it was the tango. This RAF bloke lifted me, he was very good. I wasn't very good, but I remembered it the dance steps. They could do things like that. They were sophisticated!' Janet Wilson, Cornaigbeg

For young island boys the war must, at times, have seemed like walking into the pages of a comic book story.

'I remember one time at the school in Ruaig the RAF arrived for a meeting. They parked their lorries outside the school yard there. Us boys, we all clambered over the vehicles, looking inside them. Alec MacKenzie from Milton, being an older boy than me, got into the driving seat, starting the engine and going forwards and backwards. I remember being a bit awed by this. I don't think we were discovered at all.' Duncan Grant, Ruaig

Some of the older islanders found the war a little too exciting!

'The CO [Commanding Officer] here was Preston Potts. I knew him very well; he was friendly with my father, fishing. He was a madman in a plane! He used to go over the houses here, and honest to God it was frightening! He could have any vehicle he wanted, but he had this "General Eisenhower" open Jeep and it went like the wind! Hector stayed in Heanish. Preston-Potts didn't worry about the war effort. If you were on the road, he stopped and you got a lift. There was no door on it, you just stepped into it. He was a right rascal! His favourite trick when he picked up the old fellow, he would let the clutch go and off before his passenger had a chance to sit down. And Hector was sitting in the back seat and he had his cap in his hand and his stick. I thought he was going to hit Preston Potts with the stick. And Hector got out of the vehicle and he says in Gaelic, "He's crazy that man". Neil Johnston, Heanish

Squadron Leader Preston-Potts and his wife. (MacNeill)

*'Preston-Potts was known as 'PP' or 'Preston Pans'. His face had been badly burned as a fighter pilot and he had to go to Oban to be shaved (he had a beard). No one recognised him when he came back. His family had an estate in Ireland and he used to wear an Irish kilt at social functions.'* Hugh MacLean, Barrapol.

*'Preston-Potts was desperate on mines! The man could swim like a fish. He would swim out. I saw him out there sitting on top of a mine with spanners and screwdrivers'.* Neil Johnston, Heanish.

But often there was a mutual dependence between the two communities. 'I remember very well, short of meat, maybe sometimes, but we had guns. And there were thousands of pheasants in the island at that time. And we always had a pot, if we desired one! Oh, yes! I'm sure I shot a thousand pheasants during those years. Quite a few geese too, hares. It was difficult to get ammunition, very difficult. But these RAF boys were good to us too. Maybe, "I wish I could have a brown hare, a goose for Christmas, going home on leave, maybe." They paid us in ammunition. They had plenty of it over there. We got ammunition alright! There was no hunger, no. The food that we had, it was good, really good.' Hugh MacLean, Barrapol

Many RAF men and WAAFs enjoyed leaving their base and meeting islanders.

'Sometimes we had tea with a Mrs Kennedy at Balephuil or Mrs McDonald at Hynish. Marvellous teas of poached egg, homemade scones and cakes, a real treat.' Elizabeth Lotocka, WAAF

'I remember one night coming back from a walk – one of the islanders came out to us with a glass of milk. My companions drank it, but as it was still warm, I didn't.' Mary Chaffe, WAAF

'One thing I do remember that was wonderful and came from the NAAFI was Madeira cake. My uncle Johnny, he was a great one for the NAAFI. He would bring all sorts of goodies home from the NAAFI – he was well in with the boys up at the airport. I've never since tasted Madeira cake that tasted like that. It was great altogether.' Mabel MacArthur, Hough

RAF man and local girls on a day out at Balephuil Bay. (Davis)

## CHAPTER 9

# Weather and War – 518 Squadron

For well over 100 years before WW2, military authorities had appreciated the value of meteorological information. During WW1, Royal Flying Corps biplane pilots made pioneering flights to obtain limited degrees of information on likely weather trends. During the inter-war years ships stationed in mid-Atlantic assisted with forecasting.

One of the first RAF servicemen sent to Tiree was Melvyn Howe, who had studied meteorology at university [later to become a professor]. 'Little was known about what the weather was like north of Ireland or to the west of Scotland, so they decided to put a few aircraft out here. I volunteered to go out to Rockall taking precise readings at sea level and coming up at fixed altitudes. I went out there on two occasions. I wasn't happy doing this in a very light, small aircraft [an Avro Anson]. I wasn't terribly well on one occasion. I left Tiree early in 1942. I remember going back to Oban – I was almost afraid to cross the road, I hadn't seen motor cars on Tiree at all.'

Various aircraft were trialled for Met work in the early years of WW2 before the mighty Halifax bomber was selected in 1943 for its rugged durability and relative reliability. Tiree was about to become vitally important to the Allied war effort, though the public would perhaps not have grasped the connection between 'intelligence' on weather, and success in commando or bomber raids in occupied Europe.

518 Squadron was formed in Stornoway in July 1943 and moved to Tiree two months later. They flew long range meteorological sorties over the Atlantic from September 1943 until the war concluded in 1945; almost 2 years, a remarkably long period of residency in wartime. These crews had to make arduous flights at specific heights, keeping to pre-arranged routes. They ensured that the constantly varying weather patterns were recorded and notified by code at set half-hourly intervals, throughout the 9, 10 or 11-hour sorties. In their specially adapted Halifax aircraft they gathered vital data on matters such as wind strength and direction, cloud, temperature and humidity readings. For a time Tiree also hosted a training flight for the preparation of Met crews, for duty on this island, and with other meteorological squadrons.

518 Squadron crest. The only RAF Squadron during WW2 with a Gaelic motto 'We hold the key'. The efforts of the courageous young men of this squadron most certainly held the key to many Allied successes. However, at least 48 members of the Squadron lost their lives on operations. Eleven aircraft of 518 Sqn were lost in crashes or at sea. (Cobb)

Halifax aircraft of 518 Squadron, mostly in Coastal Command white colour scheme, lined up on 'The Reef', in readiness for 'Met' sorties.

*'Instead of carrying bombs, the Halifax was fitted with extra fuel tanks to increase its range. Thermometers were attached to the nose of the aircraft, outside the Met Observer's window, so that air temperatures could be measured.'* Fred Gee.

Neville Beale served with 518 Squadron on Tiree. 'Although some Luftwaffe aircraft had the range to operate over the Atlantic, from bases in France and Norway, the main enemy [in the seas around Tiree] was of course the U-boat. It is now almost forgotten how close we came to defeat in the Battle of the Atlantic, in 1941 to 1943. 518 was one of several specialised meteorological reconnaissance squadrons operating from bases in Iceland, Scotland, Wales, Gibraltar and elsewhere. The principal adversaries faced by 518 were bad weather and engine failure. We had many Australian and Canadian volunteers. These, together with a few New Zealanders and South Africans, constituted about 40 per cent of 518's aircrew strength. We were one of twenty-eight aircrews with 518 Squadron.'

Bernard Jamieson remembers, 'I was a Flight Lieutenant pilot on 518 Squadron. We had eight-man crews, consisting of captain, second pilot, navigator, engineer, three

Leonard Revilliod on Sunday 13th August 1944 at Balephetrish, with the three McArthur sisters Anne, Grace and May. This was just 3 days before he was killed, when the two Halifaxes collided over Tiree airfield. Leonard was actually Swiss, and as that country was neutral, he had no need to volunteer, but he did, to serve in the RAF. When France fell the Revilliod family chose to leave Switzerland and settled in Edinburgh, where Leonard and his brother Herbert enrolled at Edinburgh University. Leonard was only beginning his operational tour on 518 Squadron when this dreadful crash occurred. His parents attended the funeral service and burial on Tiree. Leonard was the grandson of Tomas Masaryk, the founder and first Premier of free Czechoslovakia (1919). Olga, Leonard's mother was Tomas Masaryk's daughter. She married Henri Revilliod, a Swiss doctor. Leonard's only brother also died during the war and his mother's brother Jan Masaryk, the Czech Foreign Minister, died in suspicious circumstances in Prague in 1948, after the communist takeover. (Campbell) wireless operator/air gunners and a specialist Met Observer. These flights were made whatever the weather and were almost never cancelled. It was always possible to take off, and if the conditions were so bad that it was impossible to return to Tiree, then the aircraft was diverted to another airfield, if necessary hundreds of miles away from our base.

'At Tiree the station buildings were extensive, but Nissen hut accommodation was widely dispersed around the aerodrome. Although transport was provided for official duties, such as when flying, one normally walked and, like other personnel, I hiked many miles during my stay at Tiree. Our little group of huts was situated in a very nice position, sheltered by the sand dunes and close to the sea.

'The meteorological information obtained from these trips (codenamed "Bismuth" and "Mercer") was relayed back in code by a wireless operator, and helped to complete the weather picture for the whole of Europe. The Met squadrons covered an area which would have been a massive blank in the Atlantic, as far as the weather forecasters were concerned. On one trip we could fly through the whole of the weather systems which would take a week to pass over the United Kingdom.

'I took over the crew from a Canadian who had finished his tour in this country and we settled down well together. Standing in the open areas of tarmac one soon got used to the size of a Halifax. I remember an occasion when this aircraft did look quite overpowering. I was home on leave, and I read in the paper that a static exhibition of

'Visitors', RAF Sergeants' Mess, Crossapol. (Gee)

*'Most of the time I was there it was wet and windy and the ground soft and boggy. It wasn't wise to wander off the narrow road when going back at night; one could sink into the mud nearly up to one's knees'.* Bernard Jamieson.

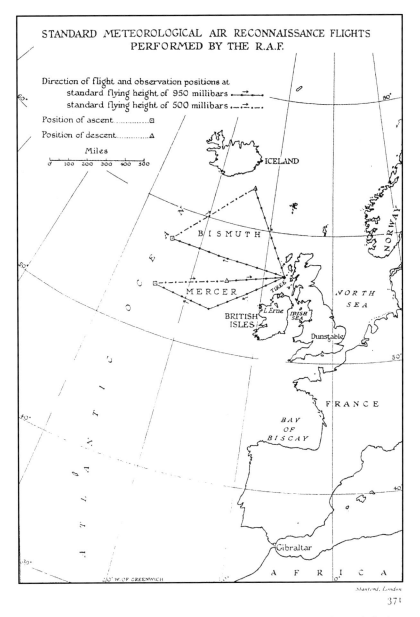

Map illustrating general direction of wartime meteorological flights from Tiree.

aircraft was being held on a bombed site in Oxford Street, London, and that a Halifax was one of the aircraft to be on display. I asked my parents if they would like to see the airplane which I flew, and they readily agreed to accompany my wife and me to the West End. There were a number of aircraft on display, but standing over them and dominating the whole site was the Halifax. In those surroundings it looked gigantic to me, and at that time I had been clambering in and out of them for several months. My mother asked me, "Well, son, which is the aeroplane that you fly, then?" I replied, "You are standing underneath it." They looked up in absolute amazement, and my father turned quite pale. They could not believe that their little boy could actually handle one of these giants!

'Shortly after I became a skipper, the squadron, which had until then suffered very little from aircraft malfunctions, experienced a spate of engine failures, of which I had my share. The aircraft were old and "clapped out", but I suspect a certain malaise might have affected the maintenance section. Confidence was not strengthened when an engine was opened up after an engine failure and found to contain a hammer, left behind by a careless fitter.

'On one occasion we were approximately 200 miles out and I was flying at the time. It was a black night. I sat with the aircraft nicely trimmed, needing only the smallest movement of the controls to keep it well on course and height. The rest of the crew were quiet, all sitting at their stations, no doubt looking forward to a good meal and their bunks. We were flying at our usual height of 1,000 feet. With no preliminary warning, the starboard engines quit; there was no noise of mechanical failure, they just stopped. I was, to be honest, taken completely unawares. Two engines stopping on one side at the same time caused a swing, which was too much to hold, and she flipped up on one wing and started a diving turn to the right. I stood on the rudder bar, trying to keep her straight, whilst winding on rudder trim to help. Just as we were down to about 500 feet and flying in the opposite direction from our course of a few seconds before, the two port engines also died. I don't think I had uttered a word, I had certainly not had time to warn the crew to prepare for ditching, and I have no idea what they were thinking or doing. For several seconds we descended in complete silence, until with under 300 feet showing on the altimeter, all four engines started again, one by one. Later, the plane's fuel system was checked and its engines stripped, but nothing wrong was found. Ten or fifteen seconds more of that inexplicable failure and there might well have been another

A crew standing below a mighty Halifax of 518 Squadron (still painted in Bomber Command colours), at Tiree airfield. (Eastwood)

*'I enjoyed flying the Halifax. It was a large aircraft, but it suited me well; I think I had a temperament suited to big planes. I had realised very early in training that I was not cut out to be the dashing fighter pilot, and after the initial awe experienced at its size I quickly felt at home with it.'* Bernard Jamieson.

Wireless Operator/Air Gunner Ron Radford, of 518 Squadron, seen during a flight. (Radford)

*'I was on "Dickie" Whittington's crew. We replaced one of the crews who crashed in August 1944.'*

*'Wireless operators/airgunners would rotate two hours on radio, two hours in mid-upper gun turret, two hours in tail gun-turret and two hours in rest position. This wasn't always carried out, especially when sightings were obtained. A U-boat fired at us just before midnight on 23rd December 1943. Due to one of our coded radio reports, we were informed later that the Navy made contact and had sunk two U-boats.' Les Cobb.*

mystery loss by the squadron. What does puzzle me now is the lack of reaction that I had to this sort of incident. Once on the ground the whole thing was treated as a bit of a joke, something to "shoot a line" about.'

Another squadron member, Brian Cass, comments on 518's aircraft, at the beginning of November 1943. 'The Halifaxes we were using were old, ex-Bomber Command aircraft and not very reliable. But in early 1944 we received brand new, gleaming white Halifaxes, each one being allocated to a crew.'

Bernard Jamieson continues, 'When I became a skipper on Halifaxes I would sometimes take a spell in the rear gun turret, which I could just squeeze into. The first time I got in while flying, I'd had no instruction at all. I climbed in and, because of my long legs, did not close the sliding door behind me. I found the power switch and turned it on. The turret swung by moving a control column and I grasped this and moved it. The turret responded far faster than I had anticipated and swung right round to its stop. I looked over my shoulder to find out I was hanging out over the Atlantic 1,000 feet below, a disconcerting experience. However cramped, I always made sure to close the turret doors after that!'

Crews developed a humour of their own to help cope with the worries they faced. Bernard Jamieson also recalled, 'If the nose of a Halifax is put down suddenly and then kept in a steadily increasing dive, anyone in the rear of the aircraft takes off and floats around, quite unable to do anything about it. We would play this trick on an unsuspecting new crew member, or any male passenger who was foolish enough to sit upon the Elsan toilet provided at the rear of the plane. The sight of a man with his trousers down, floating in a sitting position about two feet above the seat was quite hilarious. A sharp pull on the controls would then firmly seat him back down on the Elsan, where he remained stuck fast, until we regained level flight again!'

Les Cobb joined 518 Squadron just before they moved to Tiree and he has some very vivid memories of the incredible conditions these young crews had to endure. 'I was posted to 518 Squadron in July 1943. To obtain the Met information, we flew at certain times of the flight at 20,000 feet. At night, for low flying, we had radio altimeters. They would sometimes read zero, due to the wild Atlantic sea waves which were often 60 feet high. Salt spray was continually leaking into the aircraft. Our duties were observing for U-boats, convoy positioning and meteorological reports. These included cloud base

Skerryvore Lighthouse. The magnificent Stevenson-built structure, south west of Tiree, viewed from an RAF aircraft during the War. (Thornton)

*'A few miles away from Tiree was the Skerryvore lighthouse, and we used this as a check on the radio altimeter. The top parapet of the lighthouse was 120 feet above sea level, and by flying level with it a useful comparison could be made. The lighthouse keepers were used to our visits and would come out and give us a friendly wave as we whistled close by.'* Bernard Jamieson.

ceiling, temperature, icing and rain, type of clouds, wind velocity and direction, as well as general reconnaissance. We carried depth charges on many flights and U-boats could be attacked or "plotted" for the Royal Navy. U-boats often fired at our aircraft rather than dive. 518 Squadron reports led to convoy re-routings and U-boat sinkings, which must have saved many lives.

'Our navigators had to be of the very, very highest standard and we were fortunate in having Ron Toy on our crew. Can you imagine navigating out in the Atlantic, at night, no landmarks for hundreds of miles, and no stars or moon visible?

'The crofters on the island must have felt it strange to have their place taken over by so many airmen and aircraft. Their quiet, peaceful island so disturbed night and day, with aircraft testing engines and flying. But they never complained. I never met one who was unsociable; although they usually spoke in Gaelic. In the summer crofters opened their places, offering tea and home-made scones. There was an odd ceilidh which was good fun, but the few island girls were somewhat shy and wary of us airmen. I couldn't blame them! Everything was rationed – especially the tea, butter and cigarettes. Fruit and chocolate or sweets were almost non-existent.

'I must confess that I drank quite a lot in the Sergeants' Mess, more than was good for me at times (in between flying of course). Thinking back, just about all of us did. "In case of tomorrow" was our excuse.'

Oscar Gill was a crew mate of Les Cobb. 'I was a Meteorological Observer and I spent a lot of time in the specially converted perspex nose of the Halifax. I was appointed to Wilf Butler's crew. I believed none of the other skippers could match Wilf for skill and experience. He was a pre-war "weekend" pilot and had already done two tours in Coastal Command over the French coast, followed by a tour as an instructor in Training Command. Wilf was quite a small man, and because of this his landings were often somewhat bumpy – he couldn't see the runway once the tail went down, except through the side window. It was the same taking off – he couldn't see ahead until the tail came up! Oddly enough, the Halifax would fly on one engine if it could "see" Tiree. But, take it out over the Atlantic, and it could be very difficult on three engines, especially early on, when it was fully loaded with fuel.

'Our second trip out was difficult, as we were in cloud for almost all the eleven hours. When at last the cloud did begin to break we found ourselves hurtling towards a huge cliff that had 'Eire' painted on it in enormous letters! Our pilot Wilf managed to pull us up and away – just. If we had crash-landed there we might have been interned for the duration of the war. A short time later we heard one of our crews had not been so fortunate, and crashed in the same locality. We just made it back to Tiree after twelve hours and ten minutes in the air. As we turned off the end of the runway the fuel was completely gone and everything went very quiet. A tractor had to come out and tow us in to dispersal, and away we went for a good meal and a night's sleep.

'After some rough flights, to our delight we managed a trip without any engine failures, when we passed near to a U-boat which was just sitting on the surface. In the early morning half-light, he saw us first. No doubt thinking that we had depth charges and were hunting U-boats, their captain decided to open fire. So, suddenly we had cannon shells whizzing all around us. If just one had hit us it would have been the end, as we still had almost a full load of fuel (over 2,500 gallons). Wilf immediately dived straight at the U-boat and ordered "open fire", with the result that I'm sure I was able to knock the two gunners off the U-boat – something I will never forget. We could do no more – we weren't carrying depth charges. So we moved on and called up RAF Ballykelly. A Liberator came out and sank the U-boat, we were told a couple of hours later. If they had not fired in the first place they might have survived, as quite probably we would not have noticed them.

'On one occasion we were alerted to take a medical emergency over to Prestwick. An airman had an appendix threatening to burst. The weather was appalling; a cold front lying right over the area, so we were in solid thick cloud with some icing at times. Wilf thought he spotted the runway through a break in the cloud and pushed the nose down, eased the power, ready to land. Just then I shouted, "Wilf, there are houses on both sides of this runway!" It was in fact the main street of Prestwick. So we turned out to sea, got down to 100 feet and called Control to switch on the runway lights. Immediately there was a great glow in the sky and we headed for that, before they could turn them off again. The Medical Officer was apparently keeping an eye on us, for he met us when we returned to Tiree and said, "Right, that's six hairy trips in four weeks, so I'm sending you on a fortnight's leave." We didn't argue!

'On 2 June 1944 we encountered some of the worst possible weather and I was buffeted about for ten hours, gathering quite a few bruises. Wilf had to hang on in person for the whole trip as the auto-pilot could not cope. The state of the sea in that depression is very hard to describe and I can liken it only to a large pan of jam at full rolling boil on the stove. The waves were some 50–60 feet high, going in no particular direction but just bouncing up and down. The wind was lifting spray hundreds of feet into the air and the perspex nose was splattered all over with salt water. When we got back we were so relieved we carried Wilf shoulder high onto the crew bus. I got back to my bunk and I slept for 24 hours. [These were the weather conditions which we recorded, and were confirmed by subsequent crews, which helped ensure D Day was postponed from 5 to 6 June].

'On 16 August 1944 we took off from Tiree just 12 hours after seeing 16 of our colleagues killed in a head-on crash at 300 feet, with bits of burning aircraft and bodies all over the place. One of those killed was Roy (Steve) Stevenson, who joined up with me and was one of the first six Met Observers to be trained. He had married a WAAF at Tiree just a few weeks earlier. On 20 August, just four days after that crash, I was getting a lift to Woodvale, Liverpool, to get married myself. As we left Tiree it was our duty to "dip a wing" in salute over the cemetery, just as our friends were being buried. I was still crying when we landed at Liverpool.'

Ron Toy was another member of this gallant crew. 'I was a navigator on Wilf Butler's crew. Wilf was the instigator of most of the "memorable happenings". Where he led we followed, God help us! We used to fly to Limavaddy in Northern Ireland to obtain extra supplies, stuff obtainable from Southern Ireland. (Wilf was aircrew Welfare Officer). We stayed overnight in a local hotel and spent most of the evening drinking porter and whiskey. On one occasion we obtained about 30 live turkeys and carried them to Tiree in the back of an Anson. The wireless operator spent the whole flight keeping the turkeys away from the pilot and navigator. The officers, sergeants and other ranks' Mess meals were supplied, along with crew members who were going home on Christmas leave.

'Before operations we had a pre-flight meal of steak, egg, baked beans, chips, bread and butter. The baked beans caused some interesting effects when flying at 20,000 feet! During flights we had sandwiches, a bar of chocolate, barley sugars, a small tin of orange juice and a packet of ten cigarettes, plus a flask of tea. Wilf's young son used to get my orange juice.'

Ken Lunn was another early recruit to 518 Squadron. 'During September 1943, while on leave in Surrey, age 20 as a Sergeant Wop/AG, married just eight weeks, I received a posting to a place called Tiree. I could not find it in my road atlas. Its location was a mystery.

'Eventually I set off on a Friday morning on a crowded troop train to Glasgow from London, then overnight to Oban, arriving at dawn on Saturday. We then boarded a MacBraynes steamer (with two kit bags, and a huge bag with all my flying kit). What a stinking, old tug boat! We seemed to spend hours stopping to drop off sheep, pigs, cows, horses, carts and food stuff at lots of little places.

Ken was allowed to bring his wife to the island. 'I found accommodation for my wife, Peg, which was a bit primitive. Miss Wilson would not cook or wash up on a

RAF vehicles carrying coffins to Soroby Cemetry. (Dimond)

*'One lunch time during August, two Halifaxes collided over the airfield and parts of them came raining down near the NAAFI where we were having a cup of tea before going back to work. The Station Warrant Officer gave a group of us a refresher course on the slow march. On a miserable wet day we went to the burial ground in a crew bus accompanied by a low loader carrying the coffins. We did our best to slow march over the wet, uneven ground. It was a very sad day.'* Joe Sylvester.

Sunday, but if Peg cooked she was happy to eat. She was a very religious lady and blamed the RAF for the poor crops and the bad weather.

'My wife returned home, but in late July '44 I received a telegram – "Bombed out find accommodation – mummy and me arriving." I found accommodation at Calum and Mary MacPhail's, on the Balephetrish road. I have very happy memories of our stay there. My mother-in-law thought it was paradise. The six weeks she was staying on Tiree the sun never ceased to shine. Food was a problem. I can remember having the loan of a shotgun and after much effort got a goose. Could not really miss! We used to get winkles, clams and crabs from the bay. I found an old man in Scarinish and I paid to hire his boat. We split the catch.

'After my mother-in-law returned to her repaired home Peg stayed on and arranged for some vegetables and fruit to be sent from the mainland. The local children were astonished to see a banana. At that time the MacPhail family had never been to the mainland.

'Often U-boats would sink ships a few miles out and cargoes would drift in. I can remember at one stage everyone had box after box of lard, which was no good if you did not have meat or flour. Large bales of silicon/rubber were one prize, but very heavy to drag up the beach. Some of the islanders did very well, at £5 a bale. For helping we were given a sheep's head – complete with fur, teeth and tongue. We were also given a hare. Peg used to cook meals on an open fire and invite all the crew to a meal.

'On ops I saw some sights never to be forgotten – a convoy and escorts under the care of a Sunderland flying boat in heavy seas; the "Queens" (troop-carrying liners) going flat-out, often flashed us a "Good Morning" on Aldis lamps. Also, making early morning landfall at Stornoway and flying down the islands to Tiree. Beautiful, wonderful experiences.

'I can remember over Christmas period 1943 we made several attempts, in bad snow and ice, to take off from Tiree. We finally made it. Later we were diverted to a naval base and informed we were the last aircraft flying that day, in the whole of the UK!

'By the end of 1944 I had more than completed my tour of ops and was posted to Iceland. New crews had arrived on Tiree to take our place – many of them Canadians who had been trained under the Empire Air Training Scheme. In retrospect our job was not very glamorous, although it wasn't unknown to come back with a few bullet holes from either a U-boat on the surface, or from trigger happy naval personnel of unknown nationality! Four out of eight of our crew who served at Tiree survived through the war. I consider myself very lucky.

'Peg and I never stop talking about our time at Tiree. At 20 or 21 years of age we loved and lived by the day. We were lucky to be together, although the pressures it put on Peg were considerable. She never knew where I was, only that I was flying. If we were diverted, or had mechanical problems and landed elsewhere, we were gone for days. The squadron never gave information as to our whereabouts.'

Winston Dimond was one of the Australians who bravely made their way across the globe to pursue war in this Atlantic outpost. 'At Tiree, usually during the morning of the sortie, we did a half hour air test of our plane, reporting anything amiss. During the afternoon we tried to sleep. Awoken about 9.00 pm, a transport truck would take us to the Mess where the traditional pre-flight meal of ham and eggs would be served. We'd be given flight rations and then a truck would take us for a briefing and the latest weather. Take off was about midnight. We'd fly west for 700 nautical miles at 1,500 feet – about half way to Canada – on oxygen with no heating, only thick underwear and padded flying suits to try and keep warm in. Weather readings were taken every 50 nautical miles (nm). Descent was then made to sea level to take weather readings every 100 nm. After 700 nm a descent to sea level was made, then a climb to 20,000 feet. Weather readings were taken every 50 nm. On our return trip we flew due east for 500 nm at 20,000 feet. After a further 500 nm we made another descent to sea level, then returned to base at 1,500 feet, arriving home at about 10.30am (roughly a 10 ½ hour trip). By the end of the war, over 16,000 Met sorties had been flown from various airfields and 52 aircraft had failed to return.'

Maurice Foster was another of the Australians on 518 Squadron. 'My hopes of becoming a pilot were dashed when I joined the RAAF. I didn't realize there was an age limit for pilot training – 23 for fighter pilots and 25 for bomber pilots. I was 27 and too old for either. Instead I was selected for training as a wireless operator/air gunner – initially in Australia, then, like thousands of other RAAF recruits, in Canada under the Empire Air Training Scheme. After more than a year's intensive wireless, radar and gunnery training, I was posted to 518 Squadron.

'The North Atlantic, one of the world's most perilous oceans, provided vital weather information for the bombing raids and invasion of Europe. Our weather report during a flight on 1 June 1944 gave the first indication that atrocious weather lashing England would not lift by 5 June, but that it could abate enough for the invasion to proceed on 6 June. Confirmation of that information by two other Met flights later ultimately led to the decision by Allied Supreme Commander, Dwight D. Eisenhower, to delay D Day by 24 hours. On the eve of D Day Halifax L123, piloted by Flight Lieutenant Freddie Green, was ordered to make a special "Bismuth" flight to give final confirmation that the massive invasion force could expect reasonable weather. They were instructed to send coded weather reports at far more frequent intervals than normal. The accuracy of those flights undoubtedly helped save many thousands of lives.

'My first impression was that Tiree wasn't going to be a very pleasant place to do my service. Having just arrived, on the way to the base we passed the scene of a Halifax that had just tried to take off and had crashed about 200 to 300 metres offshore. There was a lot of commotion, with search lights and vehicles all over the place. Attempts were being made to rescue the crew – some of them were out on the wing. I could hear the eerie sound of whistles being constantly blown by the desperate crew members, in the freezing water, trying to direct rescuers to them in the pitch dark. Only one of the crew survived. The other seven froze to death within 15 minutes in the water. It wasn't a pleasant introduction to Tiree. The one crew member who was rescued had managed to hook his arm over a dinghy. He was half frozen when they got to him. We heard that he didn't ever fly again.

'Without the accuracy of the daily weather reporting from Met squadrons around the UK, particularly 518 Squadron, Bomber and Fighter Commands would not have operated anywhere nearly as effectively as they did, in the European theatre of war. Day in and day out we risked our lives on missions hundreds of miles out over the bleak North Atlantic. The wind was so strong one day I had to crawl on my hands and knees to get from my hut to the Mess – but planes still flew! There was an Irish doctor; we called him "Paddy", who always sat in an ambulance at the end of the runway, when the planes took off on a trip. It was comforting just to know he was there.

'On our days off we sometimes used to help the locals collect seaweed, which was one of the industries of Tiree. Evidently seaweed has a lot of iodine and they use it for fertilizer. While stationed on Tiree I met, and later married, Glasgow-born Marion

Gibson. We first met at a New Year's Eve dance in Edinburgh where the famous band leader, Glen Miller, was playing.

'Of the seven Aussies who served on Tiree when I was there, only three of us survived the war. Probably the worst day of the war for me was the time two planes collided over the top of the Officers' Mess. One plane which wasn't as badly damaged as the other tried desperately to land on the water, where they had a better chance of surviving, than if they crashed on land. But he didn't make it. He came down and blew up near the beach. There was one part of the accident that I think has affected me, in some ways, for the rest of my life. As Duty Officer I went down to the crashed plane near the runway, even though there was nothing we could do to save the crew. When I eventually had a look inside the plane I saw remains of one of the crew. What has stayed with me all these years was the sight of his badly burnt head. It was terrible. The flying conditions hadn't been that bad, but for some reason they had lost sight of each other.

'The Medical Officer was very strict on not allowing anyone flying with a cold because it was too dangerous. I remember him saying once that, because we came from a country with a much warmer climate, we Aussies should never have been left on Tiree for more than 6 months. I spent 22 months there!'

Peter Rackliff was a Met Observer with 518 and he recalls a tragedy averted, and the relief and amusing aftermath. 'On 21 November 1944, Fl. Lt. Freddie Green and his crew took off from Tiree at 10.40 am on an air test. Within minutes the starboard outer engine caught fire and the fire spread to the wing. Freddie Green decided that he would have to get down quickly, but they were some miles from the coast. Nevertheless, he made a perfect ditching and the crew were able to climb into the aircraft's dinghy. About 45 minutes after ditching a 281 Squadron Warwick dropped a spare dinghy and some extra food. Then, after nearly two hours in the dinghy, HMS *Flanders*, an ASDIC trawler, appeared, having won the race from Tobermory, and rescued the crew. Having picked up survivors, the RNR skipper was able to broach the ship's rum, and, whilst the aircrew thawed out in the engine room, they were liberally supplied with spirits and fitted out with a variety of naval gear. So a very happy and thankful crew staggered ashore at Scarinish, and were whisked off to station sick quarters. In the meantime, the whole crew of HMS *Flanders* were taken to the RAF Mess for a party. Later the RNR skipper managed to sneak into sick quarters with another jar of rum!'

Fl Lt Freddie Green and his crew, arriving at Scarinish pier, after being rescued by the Royal Navy. Some crew members are wearing dry Royal Navy outfits, given to them by their rescuers. (Rackcliff)

Peter Clark, another '518 man' was a Flight Engineer. 'Tiree – it was considered one of the worst postings in the UK. Many airmen were rather unhappy that they had landed in a place with no pubs, no shops and no girls – they did not seem to mind the lack of trees. I myself enjoyed being on Tiree for the following reasons – I met a very attractive WAAF serving as a Met girl in the ops block, who later became my wife. In the summer I spent some glorious days on Tiree. My WAAF girlfriend and I would go swimming and have a super sandy beach all to ourselves. The crofters would go down to the beach with their horse and cart to gather seaweed. I can recall the sound of the corncrakes calling each other on a summer evening.

'My first crew at Tiree consisted of five Canadians and only three RAF men, including myself. A tour on 518 consisted of 80 operational sorties, or 800 operational flying hours, whichever came first. We were always very pleased to see Barra Head or Skerryvore lighthouse approaching on the horizon after returning from a long and hard sortie. Several of the Tiree men used to hang around our Mess in the evenings. We would pass pints of beer out to them in return for boxes of eggs.'

In WW2, as in WW1, Commonwealth servicemen and women made an incredible contribution to eventual Allied victory. It seems that the presence of many Canadians in particular gave this base something of a "Frontier Spirit". Glenn Traub, RCAF, was one of the many Canadians with 518 Squadron at Tiree. He is quite open about the difficulties experienced. 'Being posted to such a remote base – well, I must say, I was not happy. I do remember the beaches, the wind, and the lack of trees. We were fortunate in that aircrew were given two weeks' leave every ten weeks. So there was certainly a break from the desolation.'

Lloyd Olsen, a Canadian wireless operator/airgunner was posted to 518 Squadron to join, at first, an all RAF crew. Before long other Commonwealth replacements began to join the crew. Like many of his compatriots, he is candid. 'My arrival on Tiree was not very inspiring – a steady downpour and the stove in the Nissen hut was almost impossible to light, as the "coal" we were furnished with was mostly shale and slag. We thought we were in a desolate place at first, but we became accustomed to the island – as

*'Colder than anywhere in Canada'* wrote Cooper Drabble of the Royal Canadian Airforce, on the back of this photo, taken of him and his friends round a Nissen hut stove. Tiree, Christmas 1944. (Drabble)

long as we stuck to the elevated cement sidewalks. We did get to sunbathe at the side of our hut in summer. Our beds were steel lattice with a "mattress" of three folding pieces of an unyielding substance. These were nicknamed "biscuits".

'At Scarinish I saw the wreckage of two Halifaxes which had crashed, on huge low-loader lorries. The aircraft were replaced but the 16 brave young men were harder to replace. A day or two after the clear-up a young boy found a severed hand clutching a wallet or pocket book. It was a Canadian, who had died in the crash. The boy turned this in at the RAF station.

'On one occasion a Halifax ditched and the crew got onto a dinghy and were rescued. This did a great deal for squadron morale. Wing Commander Morris was on this flight. He almost drowned. The aircraft was rapidly sinking and he jumped but missed the dinghy and was going straight down, because of his heavy Irvin jacket and flying gear. Wing Commander Morris wore his hair long and the Polish Met Observer reached out and pulled him into the dinghy by his hair.'

John Entwistle, AFC, has, perhaps, a more positive view of being based on a Hebridean island. Flying alongside young men from Canada had a huge impact on his post war outlook on life. 'I was very pleased to be posted to Tiree, as before the war our family had always spent the summer holidays camping in various parts of the Highlands, and in a way it was like going home. I enjoyed my time on Tiree. There is something mystical about that part of Scotland. I am not the only one to feel that way. I recall reading an account, by a submarine commander, en route from the Clyde to Scapa, in pretty bad weather. He wrote, "We battled our way north past lonely islands with magical names –Skerryvore, Tiree, Coll, Muck, Eigg and Rum, Benbecula, Shiant. I felt, as I had often felt before; that no harshness from sea, or wind, could shake my belief that this is surely the most beautiful and enchanting place in the world."

'Our crew had an Australian navigator and two Canadian Wireless Operators. We learned a lot about Canada and Australia from them and others, and that is probably what convinced me to emigrate to Canada after my demob. Whatever it was I certainly have no regrets. One time one of our Canadians got fed up with the noise we were making outside the Nissen hut and showed his displeasure by firing six rounds out of the window in our direction with a handgun.

'At the time our CO was Wing Commander Mick Angell. He was a most unusual RAF regular officer in that he would often come over to the Sergeants' Mess for a drink. The beer served in the Mess was excellent. It was light beer, very potent, and used to be offloaded from the ferry in large quantities.

'Scottish Airways brought us our mail, landing on the beach in their De Havilland Dragons, on their way to Stornoway. They would drop the mail off and land again in the afternoon on their return trip to Glasgow. I once received a letter on a Tuesday, mailed in London the previous day. I replied the same day, with my reply being received in London on the Wednesday. Things are sure different today.'

Fred Gee was an RAF man, whose appreciation of the island was enhanced through his efforts to get to know the locals. 'I was a Met Air Observer on 518 Squadron during the period September 1944 to the end of May 1945. I have mainly happy memories of my days on the island. I say "mainly" because it began badly. During the months of September and October I only completed one of my first five operational flights, on four of which we had to return to base because of engine failure or bad weather.

'Life on the camp was primitive but we soon got used to it. We slept in Nissen huts but had to walk outside to the latrines to wash and shave, and even further to the Mess for food and drink. My fortune changed in the New Year when I was introduced to the MacArthur family of Balephetrish, and then, in turn, to the two young school teachers who lived in a lonely cottage on the machair. The hospitality of those young girls was remarkable and I fear I may have endangered their reputations by calling on them so often – and leaving so late in the evening. The islanders made good cakes and baked their own bread in cottages without electricity or a mains supply of water. Illumination at night was by oil lamps and candles.'

Arthur Faulkner was a member of 518 Squadron air crew but he readily acknowledged the difficulties of servicing aircraft in the occasionally inclement Hebridean climate. 'During 1944 the Squadron cancelled only two sorties. When the island was affected by heavy snow fall the water supply to the camp was frozen, and we were ordered to conserve water and refrain from washing and shaving. We overcame this difficulty by melting the snow in a fire bucket placed on the stove in the hut. It takes a great deal of snow to get a pail of water! We even made tea with melted snow. It had its own distinctive flavour.

'The ground crews' lives were very difficult, as they had to service the aircraft working in very exposed conditions. They performed their duties extremely well and never seemed to complain very much. There was a good squadron spirit (esprit de corps). We all worked together so well under rather difficult conditions.'

The ground crew of 518 were vital for this squadron's many achievements. Joe Sylvester spent almost two years on Tiree. 'I was an Electrician with 518 carrying out major inspections on Halifax aircraft. Gum-boots were the usual footwear. We were also issued with long black oilskin macs, leggings and sou'westers. Most of us got leather jerkins, whilst squadron personnel and MT drivers, including the WAAFs, received sheepskin jerkins. Hand-knitted comforts were issued, including roll-neck pullovers, long white sea-boot socks, mittens and balaclavas. It was sometimes difficult to find two people dressed exactly alike. It was often impossible to wear field service caps due to the strong winds, and, if worn, they were usually buttoned under the chin. We were instructed to paint a large white patch on the back of our macs to make it easier for transport to see us during darkness.

'Chocolate rations, and bread and cheese (scrounged from the mess for supper when possible) had to be kept in tins or they were quickly attacked by mice. The RAF Embarkation Unit at Scarinish had created their own little pub from a Nissen hut, which they called the Pier Arms. It had a proper bar and a few chairs and tables, and was cosy and warm.'

Joe gives some idea of the tremendous efforts they made to keep aircraft flying and crews safe. 'Snow fell heavily during the winters of 1943–4 and 1944–5. During the second winter it was impossible for a time to keep the runway clear of snow, and it was compacted by running all the station transport up and down with the larger vehicles towing baulks of timber behind them. All available personnel (except the WAAFs) spent all night digging troughs down to the tarmac along the sides of the runway, so that the aircraft pilots could make out the line of the runway from the rest of the airfield.'

Despite such efforts, Joe recalls, accidents still occurred. 'During the Met Conversion training period a lot of night flying took place. One night I was lying awake in bed in our hut, which was only a few yards from the sea almost in line with a runway, when an aircraft took off. Seconds later all the engines cut out, followed by an awful bang.

The aircraft was only a few hundred yards from the shore but I don't think that anyone came out alive. This aircraft was later salvaged and laid alongside one of our hangars for a time.'

John Graham served on Tiree during the period 1943–4 and remembers both happy and sad occasions. 'My role in all this was as a Compass Adjuster. There were four of us with 518 Squadron, where usually there was only one or two per Squadron. We were kept pretty busy and compass "swinging" took place in all weathers, and often at night. The busiest time I remember was in the run-up to D Day when every plane seemed to be in the air.

'A sad event took place when one of our men was run over and killed by a Halifax under tow. I must have been going on leave and I came across his coffin on the *Hebrides* on its way to his parents in England. A pleasant lad, I remember. What a waste.

'I had a girlfriend on Tiree – quite an achievement when you consider there must have been very few of them around! I met her on the train to Oban. She was a Glasgow girl going to stay with her grandmother. I think she lived on a croft in the Barrapol area. I went to see her when possible by bike over muddy tracks, returning often in the dark. Quite frightening sometimes, but youth overcomes all obstacles. Her name was Cathy Campbell and her grandmother spoke no English. This was quite a happy time but it faded when she returned to Glasgow. Shortly after this I got a "Dear John" letter saying she was getting married and inviting me to the wedding reception at her grandmother's croft. This was quite an event which took place in the barn, dirt floor and all. An abiding memory of this day was the keg of whisky, but I have little recollection of getting back to base.'

Mostyn Tuckwell, a Welshman, was a Fitter with 518 Squadron, and also had mixed memories. 'I was in the transport workshops and worked on Halifaxes. It was a very responsible job, with no room for mistakes. I did not like being Duty Fitter as I had to sleep in the station workshops all on my own, with plenty of big rats scurrying around!

'When I first arrived at Tiree I was filled with trepidation after such a rough crossing from Oban. Once one got used to the high winds and sometimes very heavy rain, the place grew on one. The white sandy beach near the living quarters provided me and others with a fine rugby training area.'

Mrs Pat Eiles provides another fascinating insight into life on wartime Tiree. 'My husband flew as a pilot on the old Halifax bomber. He did two tours with Bomber Command. He had a couple of "prangs" and some terrible times over Germany. He was then posted to Coastal Command, Tiree. Just after we got married I got leave from the ATS and my husband came over to Oban, where we met for a few days. We had a lovely time. He managed to get a room in a croft [the Munn family] and I went to live on Tiree. My husband had a lot of nightmares in those days. He often woke up screaming in the night. Before an "op" he sometimes had a sort of premonition and went very quiet. He would not want to go flying, but had to. As it happened, in these cases, they always came back on three engines, or even two. Funny that. My husband was very young in those days, twenty or twenty-one. I was nineteen. I will always remember my husband walking home down the hill (from Baugh) in his flying kit, so tired after his "op" of ten or twelve hours, and me so happy to see he got back safe and sound. What strikes me

'Max' Bacon (left), and his crew make their way to 'dispersal' to board their aircraft for an operational flight. 'Max' Bacon, Andy Andrews, (centre), 'Rocky' Stone, (right), were all lost in January 1945. (Bacon)

*'Two of my very close pals, on 'Max' Bacon's crew, took off one night, with the Squadron CO Wing Commander Morris captaining the aircraft on this occasion. The weather was terrible. He had a choice to cancel but decided against this, and they never came back. We received no radio contact. We went out in search, but found nothing.'* Les Cobb.

most, as I think of Tiree, is the place covered in flowers, especially the colour purple. The beach was pure white sand, and we went collecting all sorts of things from the beach.

'For a time another couple also had a room with Miss Munn. He was an RAF Corporal. Coal was rationed and he and his wife often helped themselves to our small coal ration, which was stacked outside. Not a nice thing to do. We had good days and bad on Tiree. Not all the crews came back. They had to fly so low you can guess how difficult it was. That is the time Miss Munn's Bible came out. If an aircraft went missing the air force padre could be seen walking down the path from the base, to tell whoever it was the bad news. So, none of the wives wanted to see the padre. We had a very good life at the Mess, living life for today, and not worrying about tomorrow. In the winter we once had so much snow. We set off to walk to the Mess. We could hardly see, and nearly walked into the sea instead! Of course we had to return to the croft wet through. I would really love to return to Tiree one day.'

Unfortunately we will never know the fate of some aircraft that were "lost". However, one of the 518 Squadron losses we do know the fate of is that of Warrant Officer Lloyd Upshall, RCAF, and his crew. They were briefed for a 'Mercer' sortie and took off from Tiree at 06.05 on 23 January 1944 in Halifax A (LK704). Nothing was heard from this aircraft after 08.48, although they should have been transmitting Met messages. They must have experienced radio failure. The aircraft was not fitted with Loran or Gee navigation aids, and so the navigator would have been unable to check his position. They had drifted a long way south of their planned track on the homeward leg, as they were spotted flying across Donegal Bay. At this point they would have been almost out of fuel, having been airborne for over 12 hours. They must have been hoping to carry out a forced landing on a beach. At this point they almost certainly suffered engine failure or the fuel gave out. Losing airspeed, the aircraft hit the top of the cliff above Tullaghan Strand. From the Republic's official archive we have eye witness accounts of the tragic events.

*Sir,   Herewith is report from Capt. Birthistle who visited the scene of the crash.*

*I interviewed two eye witnesses of the crash, Miss Murtagh and Miss Geoghegan, manageress and assistant manageress of the Great Northern Railway Hotel. At about 18.15 hours these ladies were walking on the cliffs at the very end of the golf links when a plane passed over them flying very low and proceeded to just top the high waves and disappear out to sea; they did not notice the plane turn. They next saw it about 100 yards away and coming straight for them (18.20hrs). They screamed in terror but were unable to move; the plane crashed on the top of the cliff breaking into small pieces. The rear portion of the plane and tail fell over into the sea, which was running very high at the time. Miss Geoghegan rushed to the wreckage, which was approx. 50 yards from her, and pulled out one of the crew who was dead. She was then joined by Miss Murtagh and dragged a second man out of the wreckage who was alive, but this man died in a matter of minutes. They dragged two further men from the wreckage, but these men were also dead. They were unable to get the remaining two out as they were caught by portions of the wrecked plane. When the tail fell into the sea it caught fire as it must have contained petrol, which became alight on the waves. They could plainly see the two remaining members of the crew in the burning wreckage, as it tossed on the waves. The two bodies have not been recovered. These two ladies are suffering badly from shock and are under Dr Daly's care. They got from the hotel a bottle of brandy, for which they are not making any claim. The plane was a four-engined Halifax. Sir, I have the honour to be J. Power, Commandant Officer, i/c [in charge] G 2 Branch, Western Command.*

To commemorate the crew, family members and military representatives unveiled a beautiful memorial on the cliff top at Tullaghan Strand, about one mile from Bundoran, Donegal, in January 2004.

In contrast, Ken Lunn has an amusing memory of a finale to the war. 'On 9 May we were flying a daylight "Bismuth" sortie in good weather when there was an excited cry from one of the crew. We had come across a U-boat on the surface, which had just surrendered to a Sunderland flying boat. As we were still carrying depth charges we decided to show the U-boat crew what they might have received if they had not surrendered. As we opened the bomb doors and made an attacking approach the pilot of the Sunderland must have thought that we were about to sink his prize. Frantic flashing came from the Aldis lamp in the Sunderland and my skipper suggested that I send something rude in reply.'

It is indicative of the astonishing dedication of 518 Squadron that it may well be that this group of doughty warriors probably flew the very last operational flight of WW2 in

An airman and a WAAF brave the vagaries of Hebridean weather. *'They all deserved medals!'* (Glebocki)

Europe. Ken Walker, a navigator on 518 takes up the story. 'We took off at five minutes to midnight on 8 May 1945. (Churchill had announced the hostilities would end that day). From a navigation point of view it was a bad flight. The weather was terrible and I had great difficulties in obtaining fixes way out in the Atlantic. We eventually arrived back at Tiree after 10 hrs and 40 minutes flying, the longest flight I made. Believe me, we celebrated the following night. It was a wild night!'

# CHAPTER 10

# Tiree's Home Guard

As fears of an imminent German invasion of Britain mounted in 1940, the Secretary of State for War, Anthony Eden, broadcast a radio appeal for men between the ages of 17 and 65 to enrol in a 'Local Defence Volunteer' force at their nearest police station. Later renamed the 'Home Guard' after the LDV was nicknamed 'Look, Duck and Vanish.'

This group comprised men over the usual age of active service, those in 'reserved occupations' and those awaiting call-up. They were tasked with defending coastal locations and vital installations such as airfields, factories etc. Like so many of the volunteer units they worked long hours on top of other commitments and did so unpaid.

'These papers came for the Home Guard business. Alasdair Brown (Balephuil) was dishing out the papers and he told me this day, "I kept a paper for you." "Oh! That's alright," I said. So he gave me the paper and I filled the paper in and signed it at the bottom and sent it back. And then, after that, two men came in and we had to be at this school down at Balemartine, and there was a big meeting there that night talking about the thing before the Home Guard started. The next week after that a drill came up and they were telling us the way we were to act and slope arms and all that carry on. We got suits, you know, the khaki suit, and one of the round bonnets with a Glengarry thing on it. Everything was inside this big bag we got. And we got forty shots, two packets of shots. They were old, heavy, bolt-action rifles.' David McClounnan, Balephuil

At first the new force did its best to live up to the later 'Dad's Army' image.

'We were all in a row on the floor and these two men were showing how to slope arms, by numbers they were working. About turn and all this. We were all in a room in Balemartine School. This is where the laugh was, all the same. We were all so stupid about the thing at the start. When he would say "About turn! To the left turn! To the right turn!" So when you were turned to the right, you knew where the right was anyhow. And the old fellows, one would turn this way and the other – they were facing each

Tiree Home Guard, Church Parade, Cornaigmore, 1943.

L–R: Donald MacIntyre, Gott; Robert McMaster, Kenovay; Malcolm MacLean, Salum; Hugh Hector MacArthur, Caolas; Alexander Brown, Kilkenneth (sergeant); Donald MacKechnie, Kilmoluaig; John (Jock) Graham, Scarinish, gamekeeper (2nd Lieutenant); Donald MacLean, Vaul; Lachlan MacDonald, Sandaig; Ian McLaren, Heylipol, factor, (Lieutenant); Hugh MacLean, Barrapol; Hugh MacArthur, Balephetrish, shopkeeper (sergeant); Donald Campbell, Balemartine; Walter Hume, Hynish (sergeant); Alexander Campbell, Hynish; Hugh MacIntyre, Gott, (sergeant); Neil J MacDonald, Ruaig; Malcolm MacDonald, Mannal; Donald B MacDonald, Balephuil.

other! He would stop you like that – clap! So he would shout a bit and put the old blokes together, so he was showing them the way to turn, all this carry on! They were having a good laugh!' David McClounnan, Balephuil

One of the key functions of the new force was to man a series of look-out posts around the island.

'We had night exercises in the Home Guard, but after a day's work you weren't very fit for exercises, I'm telling you! We were on night duty once a week. And this night Donald MacIntyre was along with me (at the Reading Room, Scarinish). We were supposed to keep an eye on the shore, to patrol there. This dark night we heard something and we flattened down and saw a black shape. We thought it might be submarine crew going to sabotage the aerodrome. It was a sheep!' Duncan MacPhee, Scarinish

The Argyll estate factor was put in command, with the gamekeeper becoming one of the sergeants. The force was trained in rifle use, although several crofters were already experienced shots – as the estate, trying to protect its shooting rights, knew only too well!

'I was a great man for carrying a gun in my younger days. Jock Graham, the estate gamekeeper knew me very well and he chased me. He could have got me too, but he was kind-hearted. He let me off a few times. And I remember, he was the man who taught us to shoot at a target. And I being left-handed, the first time I was put up to shoot at the target, I was trying the rifle from shoulder to shoulder. He was behind me. It was just a put-on on my part! Which shoulder would the rifle fit? "You bugger," he said. "The same as you catch with your other gun!"' Hugh MacLean, Barrapol

Most young Tiree men were away in the forces and the Merchant Navy, but the Home Guard was a way for the men of the island community who were at home to contribute to their 'War Effort'.

Extract from Cornaigmore School log (24 November 1942), 'A concert and dance in aid of Home Guard funds to be held in school'.

For all the self-deprecating humour, the Tiree Home Guard performed a valuable role on the island during the war, keeping watch and maintaining morale when spirits might otherwise have fallen.

# CHAPTER 11

## Occasional Visitors

---

Given that Tiree was in such a strategic location, regarding the Battle of the Atlantic and the 'Western Approaches' it is perhaps no surprise that various visitors availed themselves of its facilities.

Freddie Jenkins was part of a vital unit which was tasked with getting important personnel such as engineers and equipment to the islands in the crucial early days of the Battle of the Atlantic, as Hebridean bases mushroomed but airfields were grass strips or still under construction. 'I wasn't actually stationed in the Hebrides, but for a year I was on Station Flight at Abbotsinch, near Paisley. I was a Wireless Operator on an RAF Communications Flight, the counterpart of Scottish Airways at Renfrew. In July 1942 I was awarded an extra 1'6d per day for flying duties. I doubled my pay! We used Scottish Airways civilian wireless frequency codes. Our aircraft were DH Dominies. One was kitted out as an air ambulance (donated by Lady MacRoberts). We also had a Walrus amphibian and a Dutch Fokker 22 – a gormless great thing, all wood and fabric and high wings. On start-up the ground crew had to stand by with fire extinguishers as the Wasp engines shot out great tongues of flame.

'We had to know tide states, for beach landing and we would fire a Verey cartridge on to a beach to decide the optimum landing direction, based on the direction the smoke was blowing. In some gale conditions ground crew held ropes over the Dominie's lower wings; the engines were revved up, and on a given signal, ropes were released and we bounced into the air like a cork. We turned almost immediately into the wind and the acceleration was frightening. One pilot I flew with was 54 years old. He had a log book with service in WW1 and with Imperial Airways. He had to retire the next year, and almost immediately had a heart attack, while gardening.

One of the aircraft on this enterprising unit made its last take-off from Tiree, where it had regularly called. 'As we came from Home Guard training, along the road past Isabel MacArthur's, there was this big aircraft moving around. We saw it before that on

'When we went to Tiree we often had a meal in the Scottish Cooperative Wholesale Society canteen, which catered for civilian workers building the 'drome'. Being friendly with the manager, when our schedule permitted, we brought boxes of kippers from Stornoway. So we became known on Tiree as the "Kipper Kite". Our unit flew in so low, to landing strips on sand, or in fields, that we were also called the "Rock Dodgers".' Freddie Jenkins. (Brock)

other occasions. She was behaving sort of strangely, coming down and having a look at this area down beyond the remains of these cottages, 'The Land' as we call it. We were quite used to seeing aircraft doing weird things. Here, she turned into the south and landed. At that time the runways at the Reef were not properly finished, and they were a bit rough. "We'll have to go and see what is happening here." We were armed but we didn't intend using our arms just the same. When we were approaching the aircraft this fellow came out, the captain, a smile on his face. Oh, what a pleasant chap to meet.

"Are you along to stop the invasion?"

I replied, "We're not thinking of an invasion, but is there anything wrong, when you came down here?"

"No," he said.

"And do you expect to get out of here?" I said. "You haven't got a proper runway."

"Oh, I'll get out," he said. She had come in with a load of grass seed that was to be sown between the runways, so there wouldn't be sand drift or erosion. He even took us inside and showed us the aircraft. It had a fixed undercarriage too, this aircraft, a crew of four. He was New Zealand born the captain. There as a flight engineer, he was coloured, I noticed that. They were all very, very nice to speak to and the captain started telling us,

"This kite of ours has been re-engined recently. Before now she had Daimler-Benz engines. Now she's got Pratt and Whitneys. More powerful," he said.

It was time to go then. So I shouted to the captain,

"I hope you'll be alright. There's not much of a run for you over towards Balephuil."

"Oh," he says, "I'll give you a salute as we pass." He came back over and he was away and carried on.

That plane was to kill twenty in another couple of months. Yes! I remember it well. She used to leave Abbotsinch and call on Tiree, then Benbecula and Stornoway. She was a sort of, you know, workhorse, taking materials from the mainland to different dromes in the Hebrides here. On this particular evening I saw her. I was working down the road here at the farm. I saw her coming in from the north. It turned out she was coming from Benbecula. She was a slow moving craft, very slow, a Fokker, Dutch built. In about an hour's time I heard her revving the engines and she appeared talking off. But although I knew nothing about aircraft or engines at the time, I noticed there was something not very correct about her performance. You'd hear the odd cough and plume of smoke from the engine on the starboard side. I watched her and thought, "My God! That man should land again. Find out what's wrong there." She flew on towards Iona. He was going to Abbotsinch. He had his crew and sixteen passengers aboard, fellows who were going on leave, RAF men, he gave them a lift. He must have been making for that drome on Kintyre, there's an aerodrome there yet, it was closer to him than Abbotsinch. But he didn't make it. Just off Tarbert – by this time she was well alight – whether it was the wing that crumpled or whatever happened, she crashed there. Killed the whole lot, the whole lot. She had a name, I remember the name, painted beneath the cockpit, Sylvia Scarlett, I remember it well.' Hugh MacLean, Barrapol

Wallace Campbell, an Australian, has written: 'My view of RAF Tiree was of an emergency aerodrome for aircraft patrolling the shipping lanes of the Western Approaches. I was flying in Coastal Command from RAF Limavaddy in Northern Ireland. On 13 November 1943 our crew of six (I being the navigator) were patrolling against submarines. We were just to the west of some severe weather over the Western Isles.

Dutch Fokker aircraft in RAF service. Hugh MacLean, Barrapol, witnessed the last take-off of the Fokker F 22 (Sylvia Scarlet) on 3rd July 1943. She was piloted by Fl Lt Knox, a New Zealander, accompanied by Wing Co Jones, the CO at RAF Abbotsinch, Glasgow. (McCusker)

'We had about reached Rockall when I noticed the engines ran very irregularly and lost all power as the aircraft descended fast towards the tossing wave tops skipper said to prepare for ditching. As the Wellington was about to contact the ocean-swell, power suddenly returned to the engines and the aircraft climbed towards the cloud base. At a few hundred feet the engines missed again, only regaining power in the slightly warmer air within a few feet of the water. The captain decided to abandon the operation and I gave him a course for the nearest aerodrome, RAF Tiree.

'For over two hours we progressed in this way. Dropping to the sea with no power and regaining it when almost into the water. As we approached Tiree swirling black cloud was almost on the land, heavy rain was falling and all flying had been cancelled. As we came in to land fire trucks raced along the strip behind us. We landed safely, and I still say I found it very thrilling to fly about the Western Isles area; the land of my Campbell forefathers.'

Calum MacKinnon, who now lives in Seattle in the USA, recalls a somewhat unusual 'visit' paid to his family during the war. 'This incident was told to me by my aunt, Ann Kennedy, who lived in Balinoe with her mother Christina Kennedy (*Ciorstaidh Ghobhainn*). My aunt told me the story several times in the 1950s when I was a teenager.

'During World War 2, when the island was very busy with airmen and construction workers, it was common for these men to come around the crofts asking to buy farm produce, eggs, butter, or looking for lodgings. One day, my grandmother [in Balinoe] saw an airman come to the front door and asked her daughter Ann to go and tell him that we were sorry but we didn't have any spare food to offer him. Ann went to the front door but when she got there, there was no one to be seen. She came back in and told her mother that she couldn't find anyone at the door. Her mother told her that she saw him again and asked her to go back again a second time, which she did, but with the same result.

'When her mother told her a third time that she saw the airman, Ann told her mother to go and answer the door herself. Her mother did this and came back from the front door visibly shaken and asked Ann to give her a dram to steady herself, but would not say anything else about what she saw at the front door.

'The following morning Ciorstaidh was out in front of the house feeding the hens when she saw a boy running over to the house from the post office with a yellow

Tiree under snow, January 1945. Nissen huts at Crossapol, dispersed aircraft and large hangars are all visible. (Clark)

*'My main memory of Tiree is standing on the airstrip and seeing the ocean appearing much higher than the land to both north and south.'* Wallace Campbell.

telegram envelope in his hand. Ciorstaidh took the telegram into the house and handed it unopened to Ann and said, "That's Hugh". Ann opened the telegram which explained that her half-cousin Hugh MacKinnon of the New Zealand Air Force was missing in action, presumed killed, the previous day. Hugh was the son of Donald and Mary Flora MacKinnon, who had emigrated to New Zealand in the 1920s, and he was a fighter pilot in North Africa. Ann asked her mother "How did you know this was about Hugh?" Her mother replied "It was Hugh that I saw at the front door yesterday."

Tiree, as we read in another chapter, contributed to the preparations for D Day in a crucial way. In March 1944 Combined Operations made use of Tiree airfield as part of 'Operation Kentra', one of many practice invasions designed to finely tune liaison between the RAF, the Royal Navy and ground forces. 516 Squadron (Combined Operations) operated Hurricane fighters out of Tiree to cooperate in mock attacks on landing craft, taking part in exercises around the Ardnamurchan peninsula. Halifaxes of 518 Squadron also took part in fighter affiliation exercises with these Hurricanes, and there are reports of many arguments later in the Mess, over 'who shot who down'. 516 Squadron were detached from Dundonald, Ayrshire, with ground, maintenance and signalling sections. They also used Connel airfield. Tragically, in earlier exercises as part of 'Kentra' two Hurricanes were lost, with their pilots, when they crash-landed in atrocious weather conditions, on Coll and near Ardnamurchan Point on 6 February 1944.

The passage of time, allied to the 'need to know only' approach must inevitably mean that certain wartime occurrences will remain at best unexplained, and as such some dubiety therefore lingers in the mind of the questioning. Vaul Bay was the location of one of these forever questionable incidents. Even a cursory glance at an Ordnance Survey map tells you this is quite the most unsuitable bay on Tiree for a flying boat to attempt a landing. However this appears to be exactly what FO Fife, nicknamed 'the Pharaoh of the Fjord' had to do. He was skipper of Sunderland flying boat (W4032) of 228 Squadron, based at Oban. The tragedy here is the loss of all but two of a crew of nine RAF volunteers and one passenger. The mystery is; what was this flying boat doing around Vaul Bay, Tiree, after a thirteen-hour-plus convoy protection patrol. This loss was on 4 September 1942, hard on the heels of another tragic occurrence. On 25 August 1942 the Duke of Kent was killed, when a 228 Squadron Sunderland departed Oban, picked up its Royal charge at Invergordon the next day and crashed at Dunbeath in north-west Scotland. On board the Sunderland W4032 that day in September 1942 was

Fred Nancarrow, a distinguished journalist with the *Glasgow Herald* (he had written a superb book on 602, City of Glasgow Fighter Squadron). At this time he was engaged in research for a book on Coastal Command. Nancarrow was believed to be also looking into the loss of the only member of the Royal Family to die on active service in over 500 years.

Wartime cartoon drawing of FO Fife of 228 Squadron RAF. This was drawn during a successful and eventful period he spent serving at the Faroe Islands. Fife was lost when his Sunderland flying boat hit rocks at Vaul Bay, Tiree. (John Evans, Paterchurch Publications)

Question marks appear to arise over the final moments of Sunderland W4032. Tim Wilson of 228 recalled, 'Very good friends of mine were on a flying boat which was late returning from a patrol. They flew across Oban bay around 9.00pm, requesting permission to land, I was told. I don't know why, but this request was refused a couple of times by the Controller, and they were sent off goodness knows where to. They ran out of fuel, somewhere off the outer isles and most of them perished. An MTB from Tobermory brought the bodies, in coffins on the deck, into Oban some days later.' Another squadron member of 228, Alan Lacy recalls hearing they had been directed to Invergordon, 'because of poor weather at Oban'.

According to the official RAF record, Form 1180, the Sunderland alighted in Vaul Bay and dropped anchor, but it did not hold. The skipper attempted to run the flying boat ashore, but they struck a rock and were badly damaged. Unfortunately the crew took to their dinghies and were blown out to sea. The exceptionally strong winds caused them to capsize. Two bodies were never found, one being Mr Nancarrow. The two survivors were taken to the RAF sick bay on Tiree, having been found clinging to an upturned dinghy. Hugh Hunter of RAF Kilkenneth was spending a few days in hospital that night due to a serious leg injury. He remembers the surviving flight sergeant being 'hysterical, rambling and shouting incoherently'. The pilot officer (2nd pilot) continually telling him to 'shut up', before he was eventually sedated. Perhaps the saddest factor is that the hull of the flying boat did not sink completely, to its resting place in Vaul Bay, for another couple of days.

Another perspective on visitors to wartime Tiree comes from William Smith of 280 Squadron. 'A persistent rumour was that U-boat crews landed and made foraging trips on the island.' However William also has another memory which is even more fascinating. 'There were tales circulating during my time on the island that Tiree was to have been a bolt-hole for the government and other important people to escape to Canada, in the event of the Germans occupying the mainland.'

Does this revelation go any way to help answer an often asked question in relation to one prominent, surviving wartime building; 'A Fighter Sector Control block? What, out in the Atlantic?'

'The reason they built the Fighter Block was Tiree was to have a Fighter Unit, principally with the intention of defending the airport. It was used for three or four months. Half of it was underground to protect it against bombs and all that.' Angus Munn, Heanish

David Collison was with the RAF at the Kilkenneth radar site. 'At one point we were told "Expect a big kerfuffle any day. A huge number of planes might arrive at any minute. They will need to refuel." There were avid rumours that if the Germans invaded it would be Winston Churchill and members of the Royal Family. We were told they would set up government in exile in Moosejaw, Saskatchewan.'

'They were going to fly them here [the Royal Family]. They would be picked up by American long-range aircraft. From here they were bound for Iceland, then Canada. That is what we were told. There was a lot of speculation at the time.' Hugh MacLean, Barrapol

On the island, in the years after the war, builders who had access to the old operations block on the airfield site spoke of a metal-lined underground chamber, with a tunnel link to the runway.

Thankfully these emergency measures were never required and Tiree went on to play an important, if not quite so spectacular, role in WW2. It seems only logical that there would have been plans to evacuate key personnel from London in the event of invasion, and fighter aircraft support would have featured. Crossing the Atlantic 'in one bound' only really materialised later in the war and so re-fuelling would have been essential.

One well-informed islander has the last observation:

'It flooded like a well every time it rained. I remember playing in the Fighter Block in two or three feet of water. You went down the stairs into this fairly large room and then there was another tier, except that was concrete. They had big maps and pointers. I remember the odd fighter coming in. Sometimes an aircraft carrier passed here and twenty of them would come in and land on the airport as an exercise. We were all playing in it, putting headphones on. We were all fighter pilots. No one ever came in and said, "What are you doing in here?" It was just abandoned. These metal lockers were there by the hundred, helmets, gas masks. They just walked out and abandoned it, typical government thing. They didn't even lock the doors, a waste!' Angus Munn, Heanish

# CHAPTER 12

## Women in the Ranks – WAAFs

There was a famous WW1 poster which asked 'What did you do in the war, Dad?' If you ask the surviving, wonderful, mature ladies who were WAAFs (members of the Women's Auxiliary Air Force) on Tiree in WW2 what they did, they might answer 'Wild Atlantic Adventurous Females'. This branch of the RAF was formed by volunteers in June 1939 and subsequently young women were also 'drafted' from December 1941. It is true to say there was always a degree of 'glamour' associated with this branch of the services.

Janet (Houston) Mowbray was one of the true pioneers, one of the hardy breed of young women who first ventured west to this wartime Hebridean outpost. 'I was a WAAF in admin, my first posting being to a balloon barrage station at Bishopbriggs, in January 1941. Then I was commissioned in September and posted to Oban. Our office was in the Argyll Hotel. In June 1942 I went to Tiree and was there until the runways sank!

'Thanks to my diary notes I have the following record. On 19 June I got a phone call with my posting to Tiree to start the WAAF section. 23 June we sailed. It was a nasty day and we sat on deck next to the funnel to try to keep warm. There were never very many WAAFs there in 1942. I think maybe about 40 at the most, and about 2,000 airmen. Sometimes the girls would be asked to Scarinish to the radio station to a small dance in the NAAFI (music by gramophone). The WAAF officers were Code and Cypher (C&C) apart from myself. I was Admin, but I helped out with C&C if they were busy, or when someone was on leave. The CO was Group Captain Tuttle, who loved to fly. It was very difficult to catch him in his office.

'I had a bike for transport. At this time there was no battle dress for WAAFs and it was very difficult getting on to a man's bike with a tight WAAF skirt. This led to me being sent back to Oban to hospital, as I managed to pull a cartilage. I made the journey on an Air Sea Rescue Launch. I eventually returned to Tiree on 7 July. 1942 was a very wet summer and eventually we were told that the runway was sinking and the station

WAAFs outside Nissen hut entrance in 'appropriate attire' for Tiree. (Clark)

*'Most of the winter, wellie boots and black MacIntosh coats were all the rage. The gales made it impossible to walk on one's own, so that it was a case of three or four people struggling against the elements together. Summer wasn't so bad – long hours of sunshine with no shade whatsoever.'* Sandra Duncan.

would be put on a care and maintenance basis. Operations were closed down and all WAAFs were posted on by November 1942.'

It was sometime before the female contingent was built up again. Leanora Burden was part of this (second) deployment. 'I was stationed on the Isle of Tiree in 1943. I was at that time a driver MT and used to transport the aircrew to the runways. Tiree was a strange place for WAAFs to be because we were outnumbered by airmen 100 to one. I think the natives resented us being on their island. Looking back I don't blame them. Our billet which was a Nissen hut held 32 WAAFs.

'The great highlight of the week on Tiree was a visit to the camp cinema. I remember we used to sit on hard wooden benches, but it did not seem to matter as we were transported to another world. The other diversion was the good old NAAFI, where we used to sit for "Housey, Housey" [bingo] and chat over a "cup of char and a wad". I have never tasted tea before or since like that tea. They used to say it was "doctored"; supposed to quell desire for the opposite sex! I don't think it worked.

'When I was posted away from Tiree the boat stopped at Tobermory to pick up passengers. Amongst them was a woman named Unity Mitford. She got into conversation with my friend and I. She said one of her sisters was married to Sir Oswald Mosley, whilst another was a famous writer and so on. Unity Mitford went on to say (which I did not believe and thought she was "shooting a line") that she had known Adolf Hitler very well indeed and had stayed with him at his famous hideaway, "The Eagles Lair". Also, she had tried to commit suicide and shot herself in the head and that the bullet was still lodged in her skull! My friend looked at me and said, "Shall we go to the ladies room?" We excused ourselves, we both thought the woman was weird or mad or both. After the war I discovered it was all true.'

Margaret Briengan was not unusual in that she viewed her war service as a great adventure. 'I was posted to Tiree from 18 Group HQ at Pitreavie Castle. I'm afraid I didn't know where Tiree was – I'd never heard of it. Much to my surprise I enjoyed the boat trip. I was the only WAAF on board. There were RAF men and aircrew, but they seemed to sleep most of the trip. I will always remember that day – it was early spring and the sun was shining and the water was crystal clear. There was an air sea rescue launch in Scarinish harbour. The scene was beautiful; the colours – it was like a picture, and I thought "I'm going to like it here".

'Entertainment was good. There were dances in the Sergeants' Mess. The winters were awful. You would get all made up to go dancing and go outside. The rain and wind, it was like ice cutting into your face. When you got to the dance, it was out with the make-up and comb all over again. But we were young then and it didn't bother us.'

Sandra Duncan was another young WAAF who viewed this island posting positively. 'I really did like Tiree, it is a lovely island. It was just so different from being on a very busy, big operational station. But social life was practically non-existent. When I went out with another few WAAFs we were among the first women who had been posted there. I was the only one who wore battle dress and trousers and this did nothing to endear me to the women on the island.

'I was a Technical Store Keeper (LACW). I was actually discharged in February 1944 after I contracted chest trouble at Tiree. Badges were issued to personnel that were invalided out of the forces, so that we could wear them when we went out into "civvie street", and let people know that we had served and were not dodging the call up. Believe me we needed them, as we did get a lot of badgering.

'Recently I saw surfers at Tiree on TV. It was the first time I had seen the island without Nissen huts, petrol installations, and all the heavy ground equipment which made up an air station. The pictures make it look so peaceful. It's no wonder the islanders were antagonistic towards the RAF.'

Mary (Kent) Chaffe recalls her time on Tiree. 'I was a WAAF serving at Tiree between February 1944 and February 1945. I was then LACW Kent and was a cook in the Sergeants' Mess, being one of several cooks and waitresses attached to 281 Squadron. On arriving at Tiree, the physical training corporal told us to form twos and we had to march to every section to be signed in on the camp. We passed a crowd of men at one spot. All we got were whistles and calls. The NCO said, "It's alright girls they haven't seen a woman for a long time." You see, at that time there were only about fifteen women on the camp.

'Once I saw our Sergeant cook talking to a pilot in the kitchen. I looked into a very disfigured face; the poor man had no eyebrows or lashes, he had been terribly burned. He was doing office work at Tiree whilst waiting to go back to hospital for further skin grafts. These men must have suffered agonies.

'The winter months were very rough and blustery. We often had a job to walk to work! There were a lot of wooden posts with wire running through them, so we held on to the wire as we walked along. We were issued with black, glossy raincoats and sou'westers. I never felt so well in my life as I did on Tiree … Once a week we had to stay in our billets all evening. We were expected to do any mending that needed doing and give the hut a good clean.

'We had a bakery on camp. We made all our own bread, also bread rolls and fancy cakes for the Officers' Mess. We sometimes let the islanders have bread. (We never did night duty. Men cooks did that because of rats on the camp). One new girl was a parachute packer. She slept next to me. She mixed in very well. When we got to know her, we used to sing to her "Parachute packing mama."

'The worst thing that ever happened on camp was the two planes that crashed in August 1944. I saw all the debris coming down. We had just eaten and were in the WAAF rest room. We heard a terrible bang. We opened the window and looked out. At first it looked as if wreckage would hit the Mess. The phones were ringing then, and a lot of rushing around. Other air crew helped the medical officer to search for bodies. These were spread around some miles. Some were in the loch. The MO got stripped and went in for them. Everyone was very silent that night. Days after I saw the funeral go by. The coffins were in RAF lorries and each had a flag covering them. As they passed by I stood and saluted, then went on my way. Someone must have made a big mistake in the control tower.

'We were in our billets one evening at Christmas. It was nearly time for lights out. Suddenly over the tannoy a voice said "Hello all you little WAAFs, I hope you are safely tucked up in bed". It was one of the WAAF officers – I think she had been "celebrating" too much.

'When January 1945 came in, so did very bad weather. Aircrew had to go out to help clear runways. They were iced over. We cooks had to work on to supply hot drinks and food. It was about 1.00am when we walked down the road to bed. We were up again about 4.30 the next morning. A few weeks after we were told we were leaving Tiree. None of us wanted to go. We girls were flown off the island. I had to sign a paper to say I did this at my own risk. There were three waitresses and three cooks. It was a small plane we went in, only a seat for the pilot. We had to stand for the flight one in behind the other.'

Barbara Clark was a WAAF on Tiree when RAF Tiree began to be developed significantly in 1944. 'Four of us WAAFs in the Met office at Tiree met, and eventually married, aircrew, so there must have been some magic in the air! The Met office was in the Ops Block and was manned twenty four hours a day. We worked eight hour watches – plotting synoptic charts, sending up balloons to record wind speed and direction at height, cloud base etc. Also we made hourly records of barometric pressure, temperature, visibility, types of low, high and medium cloud, as well as daily records of rainfall and sunshine. I remember the wonderful sunrises when we came off duty and the great clarity of air when we could see islands to the south, 30 or 40 miles away. Of course we experienced the gales and blizzards too.'

Georgie Porazka, an English girl, met her Polish husband-to-be on the island. 'Tiree, it was a magical place, friends made there are still friends after over 60 years. I arrived on the island in January 1944. There were about 100 WAAFs and well over a thousand men, so we had a great time! We five Met WAAFs got on so well we wanted to stay together, and so volunteered for Tiree despite tales of rain, wind and isolation. But we were never bored. We had leave every five months. It took me nearly two days to get home to Suffolk, but it was worth it. I booked a seat on the De Havilland Dominie [mail flight] – over £4 but a bargain. They piled mail bags all around me. It was wonderful looking out over the sea and lochs. At Glasgow the plane was so small we taxied into a hangar, just like a garage.

'An absorbing job; very long hours, but when you are young you can take it. We loved the island; wonderful scenery and fresh air. We swam from March to October. The Gulf Stream kept the water warm. Later we had bikes and, instead of walking, we cycled to the Mess, to the Ops block, and on pleasure trips. One terrible day two Halifaxes collided; 16 men were killed. We had a big funeral parade. I vividly remember the stretchers, stained with blood even after scrubbing, put out to dry outside the sick bay.

'Once we burnt our hut down! To warm us, someone had poured engine cleaning fluid on to the old stove. Screaming, I ran over the burning lino to escape. Two weeks in hospital; no hut, no clothes, nothing left, except my engagement ring and pyjamas.

'I had various boyfriends; then met Tony who was Polish. His adventures, getting out of prison camp in Poland and then across Europe were horrendous. We courted for ages. My parents were aghast but we married in June 1945. I then went back to Tiree alone, as Tony had done his tour of flying. But after three months the married girls were released.

'There was a light heartedness about us all at Tiree. The young pilots were incredibly brave and clever. I keep in touch and get news of old friends, even in Canada, but it is all so sad when colleagues die. I cry watching the Remembrance Services on TV.'

Jane Inglis was among the last young women to serve on Tiree in the closing stages of the war. 'Having spent two years wireless operating underground at 18 Group HQ, Pitreavie, near Rosyth, I volunteered after speaking to a WAAF officer, who had just returned from Tiree. It was just magic. Everyone on the island was tanned, and because

WAAFs Georgie Porazka (left), Barbara Clark (right) and a friend celebrate a 21st birthday party in a Nissen hut on Tiree. (Porazka)

Finale of an RAF show at Crossapol Hall, 1944.

*'Apart from long hours on duty we had a classical music club, leather work class, dress making, play reading. Also ENSA came, and Perth Rep company too. We had cinema about two evenings a week.'* Georgie Porazka.

of the sun and wind, the older uniforms had turned a shade of green. The white sandy beaches, jade green/blue sea and the wild flowers were so beautiful.

'As the war neared its end, crews from overseas countries were starting to leave Tiree, but the social life went on. We had overseas priority films every week and children would come up to ask us what would be on at the cinema that night. They were so nice and polite. All the islanders were friendly and most joined in. I remember the dance in one of the hangars on VJ night. We had an excellent pianist and a talented concert party "The Tireans".'

Elizabeth Lotocka, like many WAAFs, accentuated the positive. 'I was on Tiree from about April to September 1945. I was a driver in the MT section, driving mostly air crew coaches and lorries. Being taller than most of the other girls, I could reach the pedals on the large transports. I found the island enchanting. I worked 24 hours on, 24 hours off duty. Once the night flights were in we could sleep. If you wanted the "bright lights", the posting was a penance. But if you enjoyed an open-air life, Tiree was paradise.

A corncrake used to call from a field near the WAAF quarters. I bought a canoe from a sergeant, who made it himself and was leaving the island. A friend and I used to go out in it and once saw a huge whale or shark. Also, lots of gannets diving for fish. We used to collect the green Tiree stone, which the chaps would polish and make into ornaments in the workshops.

'There were quite a few dances. A coach was sent all around the island to collect any locals who wished to come. The food was rather dull, a lot of local mutton. Because of the lack of fresh fruit and vegetables we had large bowls of ascorbic acid (vitamin C) tablets by the tea urns. Our WAAF quarters were Nissen huts. The "ablutions" seemed quite far, so we used to have a quick wash and teeth clean at a standpipe outside our hut.

'It was said that when 'The Reef' was closed down, the Chief Engineer Officer, a rather tough character, was in tears in Scarinish when he left. His name was Preston Potts.'

*'I had every other day off to explore and it was a beautiful summer. A friend and I used to swim a lot in Balephuil Bay and Balephetrish Bay. We used to take picnics. We could buy eggs from the islanders, and scrounge bread from the cookhouse.'* Elizabeth Lotocka. (Michael Olizar – Sikorski Museum)

CHAPTER 13

# Air Sea Rescue

Tiree had RAF air sea rescue, and marine craft personnel ('Web footers') with their launches, based at Scarinish at different times during WW2. Air sea rescue was also carried out from the sky. This was a little-known, but crucial, ingredient in the Battle of the Atlantic. 280 and 281 Squadrons RAF both spent periods on the island.

Tom Currie remembers. 'I was part of 280 Squadron detachments posted to Tiree during 1944–5, using Warwick II aircraft, with airborne lifeboat and Lindholme rescue gear. When we dropped the lifeboat a small drogue parachute deployed, followed by six other parachutes, shortly after release. Hitting the sea triggered a mercury switch, which fired a sea anchor into the sea. Once she was settled on the water, switches activated two rockets carrying about 700 feet of kapok line, terminating in small floats in the

A Warwick aircraft in flight, showing the underslung lifeboat. (Hall)

*'Once, as we went out over Ben Hynish, we experienced a violent shaking throughout the aircraft. Looking out on the starboard side of the plane, maybe 75 yards away, there was a Halifax commencing its approach. The buffeting was the slipstream of their four engines. One second sooner by us or by them, would have meant a total disaster. We continued our mission with unspoken relief that we were all still in one piece.'* Leo Crowther.

RAF Air Sea Rescue launches regularly made use of the facilities at Scarinish Pier during WW2. (Stoker)

rocket nose. People in distress therefore had 1,400 feet of line to catch hold of, to pull themselves towards the lifeboat. Supplies of food, water and tablets were carried in the boat, which had two Britannia "Midi" engines, and could also be sailed with the sailing gear carried.

'The idea was very good, especially if the survivors of an aircraft or ship were fit enough to get the sail up. Survival packs of various things like glucose tablets and Benzedrine [amphetamine] were included, along with fishing gear and mirrors for signalling. There was a hand-cranked radio transmitter and the antenna could be also attached to a kite, wind permitting.

'During May and June 1945 the Tiree detachment [at that time 5 or 6 Warwicks] were involved in air sea rescue patrols to cover repatriation movements to Canada and the USA via Iceland, Greenland and Goose Bay. The aircraft were probably full of US airforce, army and navy blokes going home on leave or demob.'

A Lindholme Lifeboat dropped from a Warwick aircraft of 281 Squadron. (Currie)

*'Pilot Officer Stevens crew flew towards the Shetlands on an ASR mission. Attempting to land at Sumburgh they struck a radio mast and sliced about 10 foot from the wingtip. Stevens managed to keep the aircraft on an even keel and landed at Wick. We called them the crew "living on borrowed time."'*
Bob Anderson, Flight Mechanic, 281 Sqn.

Ron Hall explains. '281 Squadron began life at RAF Thornaby towards the end of 1943, before moving to Tiree. I was a nineteen-year-old sergeant Compass Adjuster. On the Squadron we had a number of Warwick aircraft, carrying lifeboats. My job was to adjust the aircraft compasses, so that the crews could fly a correct course and find their way back to the island. I was on the top rate of pay for a sergeant of 10 shillings, or 50p a day!

'Tiree was a notorious "hard" station, where the stay was said to be limited to 18 months and supposed to be the site of any last stand against the Germans, should they invade Britain. Our arrival at Tiree was memorable. An onshore gale kept us about one hundred yards off Scarinish pier for 24 hours – no heat, no food and nowhere to sleep. When we got ashore, the billets were no better! The fires, lit the day before to welcome us, had gone out, and the Nissen huts were freezing.

'We also had a Sea Otter seaplane, which was small and only of use when the wind was not blowing. That was not very often in Tiree. Our Squadron once rescued a German submarine crew. But only once!'

William (W. H.) Smith was another of the ASR contingent. 'I was posted to 281 Sqn on Tiree. My job was in the workshop servicing airframe parts such as wheels, brakes, hydraulic ramps and motors. There was very little ceremony, no parades, and more like a job in civilian life. The feeling of isolation is what I remember most.'

Ken Salt of 281 Squadron was also based on Tiree. 'Our accommodation on the island was Nissen huts sleeping 24 men, with a central stove and one common toilet. If you ventured out in the night, your first encounter would be a cow's head, immediately outside the door, sheltering from the wind. The washroom, canteen and NAAFI were over a mile away, and the aircraft dispersal points a further mile, so all your daily needs were carried with you from early morning until return late at night to bed. We wore many layers of clothing, including a leather jerkin, and commonly moved about the airfield in 'strings' – one holding the coat tail of the one before, and the leader wearing glasses, as he alone could look into the wind. Making fine adjustments inside the engine nacelle [housing], when the engine is going full blast and the propeller is only six inches from your nose and in bitter weather, is no joke.

'Off duty, a walk to Balemartine for a cream tea (there were one or two private eating houses) was as far as I went. I do recall that there was a good dance band, with a very good trumpet player. The NAAFI was the only centre of "culture" on the island at the time.

RAF groundcrew checking equipment and rockets on ASR lifeboat, carried beneath a Warwick aircraft. (Hall)

*'The lifeboat was almost as long as the fuselage and was well provisioned. It was dropped from some 1000 feet. This saved many lives.'* Ken Salt.

'Our nearest soccer opposition was at Benbecula, a short flight away. On one occasion we played an away game of badminton against the local team at Scarinish, hitting the shuttle through the low roof rafters all the time. I went to church one Sunday, only to find it all in Gaelic, not surprisingly.'

Charles Hallett found himself at Tiree towards the end of the war. 'I served for a few months in 1945 on Tiree on ASR detachment. We flew from Tiree to halfway to Iceland and another crew flew the remaining distance from Iceland to halfway to the Hebrides, rendezvousing at a Royal Navy destroyer, which was on duty for approximately 6–8 weeks at a time.

'Before being posted to Tiree, I had been in Bomber Command. On my final "op" we were shot down. I was the only one to escape, first with the help of the French Resistance, and then by Airey Neave [a British officer who had escaped from Colditz]. On return I was debriefed in London, and sent home on leave. The RAF was stepping up ASR activities, so I found a niche for myself in September 1944.

'On our first trip we thought we would give a destroyer a buzz, indulging in a little low flying around the ship. But we felt very sorry for those sailors, stuck in this one forsaken spot, just to provide aerials on which the Americans could do some direction finding. So we promptly contacted the naval authorities at Gourock, asking if we could deliver the sailors' mail, but this was refused. So we then set about collecting all the old magazines and newspapers in the Mess and dropped them in a container by flare parachute to the waiting ship. This was very much appreciated (and they got to keep the silk parachutes!).

'As for Tiree, I hated it at first, but then came to love the place. As it was the summer months of 1945 I saw it at its best. Also, a nice WAAF from Glasgow, who was stationed there, helped considerably in my appreciation of the island.'

Leo Crowther writes 'Tiree was probably the only place I would like to see again in terms of my wartime postings. I was a wireless operator/air gunner on the crew of Flying Officer Johnny Rapp, possibly with the first ASR detachment arriving there in February 1944.

'Ourhut's location on Crossapol shore was something to cherish – the sea some 30 to 40 yards away, with a beautiful sandy beach and a grassy bank, the only features separating us from the vast expanse of the Atlantic Ocean. If anyone ditched, or maybe one of 518 Squadron's Halifaxes had engine failure, then it was important for us to get airborne as quickly as possible. Despite being an air sea rescue aircraft and crew, we too faced the very real possibility that the ocean might become our final resting place.

'On one occasion we had been briefed to patrol a search area some 500 miles out, which was towards the prudent limit of our Warwick's endurance in terms of fuel, particularly as our search area had to cover something like 100 square miles. We had barely commenced our search when we were alerted by skipper Johnny Rapp that our hydraulic system had begun to leak oil. We began by trying to lighten the plane's load by jettisoning every bit of movable gear which would fit into a chute, down which we normally pushed our flame and smoke floats. We were also losing height gradually, and watching the air speed getting too close to stalling for comfort. We altered course for our nearest landfall, which was Northern Ireland, more in hope than expectation. Our predicament by now had lasted some three hours and I remember thinking when we passed over an outgoing convoy that I probably wouldn't mind parachuting into the sea now, with all those ships below us, our chances of rescue might be pretty reasonable!

'We chose to land at Ballykelly. Our landing gear and ailerons would not operate and a belly flop was our only option. We barely had any fuel left. We crashed with one big bump. The undercarriage collapsed, our propellers bent into all shapes, and our out-of-control aircraft hurtled down the runway at something like 90 to 100 knots. Turf appeared inside the belly of the aircraft with the grinding rattle of metal. We finally stopped, totally unscathed, due to following correct crash procedure. The skipper inquired after our welfare via the intercom system. A deathly hush was his reply. By now we were all outside waving up at his cockpit, much to his, and our, relief. Johnny received a commendation, well deserved. A plane arrived from Tiree to bring us back to our home base. "We heard you blokes had bought it at Ballykelly". And thus we again got on with the job.

'Our work all too often produced little reward. With the vast expanse of ocean to be covered, and the atrocious weather we might encounter on arriving at our search areas, even four pairs of eyes, pilot and three manned gun turrets, had little chance of success.

'However, one successful rescue gave us great pleasure at the time, but a little sadness later. We were alerted to a Fairey Swordfish ditching with its two man crew. Approximate location was south of Tiree and north of the coast of Ireland. We commenced to "square search" the area. Suddenly we spotted a dinghy in the sea below us, quite small, designed for one person only. There was another chap in the sea hanging on to the dinghy. We made tracks to a destroyer, communicated by Aldis lamp and then retraced our route,

Photograph taken from a 281 Squadron ASR Warwick aircraft from Tiree, June 20th 1944. RN Destroyer pulls alongside Fairey Swordfish crew in dinghy. (Crowther)

222 TIR 281 20 JUNE 44 6½" RESCUE OF SWORDFISH CREW 5527N 0839W 50' X3.5

laying smoke floats behind us from the destroyer to the dinghy. In a short space of time the destroyer arrived, put out a small boat and took the pilot and his observer on board. We returned to base with a great sense of satisfaction at a job well done. Unfortunately, we later heard from the Navy that despite our and their efforts, one member of that crew had died in hospital, which was a sad ending to our mission on that day, 20 June 1944.

'During our lazy days by the beach we would often encounter groups of Italian POWs, apparently quite happy to be out of the war by 1944. [Their demeanour was quite different to that of some of the German POWs we encountered later]. These chaps were used on tasks around the camp – in our case cleaning our rooms, keeping the ablutions clean and generally almost acting as "batmen". I was always impressed by their cleanliness and smart, disciplined bearing and even behind the wire of their compound they could be seen doing gymnastics and other physical exercises.

'With the exception of VE Day, some of my happiest days on the island were the various sporting activities we enjoyed. We were fortunate to have a first class sports officer in charge of the gym and all the other recreational activities – Flight Lieutenant Stan Squires, a Surrey cricketer by profession, and an all-rounder for the England team after the war. Stan was a lovely man. He even had an indoor cricket net installed in the gym.

'I must pay a tribute to those ladies and gentlemen who had left their own homes to join ENSA concert parties. I always felt that the travelling concert parties were to be admired for their spirit and determination to visit the services bases such as our own. With a couple of hours of singers, comedians, sketches, some good some not so good, doing their little bit to entertain us.'

# CHAPTER 14

# Britannia Ruled the Waves, MacBraynes the Seas

It is quite impossible to tell a tale of Hebridean life without acknowledging the infinitely important role of the steamer, the ferries, the mail boat – refer to them as you please. The illustrious David MacBrayne Ltd, as was, is integral to this wartime adventure, as one might imagine, though there were at the time, other companies plying these waters, such as McCallum Orme & Co. Vessels such as the *Hebrides* and *Clydesdale* were, shall we say, in the twilight of their service to the Hebridean communities, and were much-burdened by additional wartime demands. The *Lochearn* was greatly admired for her sleek lines but schedules did not exactly adhere to the strictest timetables. The following recollections may be a mixed bag, but they are always voiced with just the merest trace of affection. Let us begin with the young ladies of the WAAF.

Elizabeth [Gilbert] Lotocka has typically 'mixed' memories of the sailings. 'I did the journey by train from Glasgow to Oban two or three times (in 1944), a beautiful journey. The train used to arrive late evening at Oban and I stayed at a large hotel, where a quite elderly receptionist used to take me in and give me a sandwich and cup of tea, and would wake me in the morning. Then it was a quick dash along the front to the quay, where MacBrayne's boat left at 6.00 am, with assorted cargo on deck; sheep, chickens and maybe a post office van. After Ardnamurchan Point the sea got really rough. But there was always a welcome transport to take us to the Reef.'

Mary (Kent) Chaffe has powerful recall of the prevailing attitudes of this time. 'The boat to Tiree was very primitive, at least I thought so. We had to sit in long narrow compartments, with wooden benches each side. The girls sat on one side and airmen the other. As we went on one journey the weather became quite rough. Eventually we arrived in the bay, but it was too rough and choppy to land. We were told we would be out all night. An NCO arrived to tell us we had to go in with officers and NCOs. This we protested against. We were happy just to sit and chat to the airmen. But orders were orders and we had to go. We spent the night on the floor, our greatcoats acting as pillows.'

Men from 518 Squadron RAF on board the *Clydesdale* sailing from Oban to Tiree. (Eiles)

*'The steamer that took me to Tiree, with its tall red and black funnel belching forth clouds of smoke, and its gleaming, pulsating engines thrilling the heart, whatever they might be doing to the stomach, was a real boat. It had a proper main deck too, tempting passengers towards a real stern and we could peer down at the oncoming waves.'* Frank Hamp.

WAAFs and airmen en route to Tiree onboard *Lochearn* during WW2. (Anderson)

Leonora Burden remembers 'When I was posted to Tiree the small boat that sailed out of Oban was hardly seaworthy; I don't know where they got it from but it bobbed about like a cork. The result was nearly everyone was very seasick – even some of the crew! I spent my voyage prone on the floor of the ladies room and thought I would die.'

Les Cobb, who was aircrew with 518 Squadron also has strong memories of the ferry:

'Getting to Tiree was a long tiring journey overnight by train to Oban. The last good stop was at Stirling where "Jock's Box" would provide us with a free cup of tea and a wad (bun).

'Blackout was strictly in force from sunset to dawn on this hazardous train journey, with possible rock falls. We boarded MacBrayne's cattle boat departing about 8.00 am. In summer, maybe May and June, the weather was really lovely and everywhere looked beautiful. But sometimes the animals, which were always aboard, were sea-sick. The smell was vile. Facilities for a meal were awful; semolina was always available!

'On one occasion (February 1944) the MacBrayne's boat couldn't anchor at Tiree because of terrible weather conditions, and the ship's mate was unable to make contact by radio. I was sent for and operated an Aldis lamp and communicated to shore, stating we were going to anchor in a bay off the island and shelter till the weather improved. My reward? The mate was on duty for two hours and off for two. So I had his bed the alternate two hours, which was much better than sitting on a wood frame bench!'

Joe Sylvester, also of 518, recalls, 'On the ferry we would sometimes leave the ship for a few minutes whilst she was berthed at Tobermory, and dash up to the Mishnish Hotel for a couple of whiskies. Once, when returning to Tiree, the ship had just left the pier when two RAF men came running down the road from the direction of the Mishnish. The captain refused to return for them and they were left behind, to the accompaniment of laughter and cat calls from those of us safely back on the ship.

'One afternoon, when returning to the island, the captain decided that the wind was too strong to risk berthing at Scarinish pier and the ship turned back and took shelter inside the entrance to the Sound of Mull, where we stayed anchored overnight. We spent a cold, miserable night, without food or a bed, as the little accommodation that was available was allocated to others than ourselves. However, in the early evening a few of us saw a long line of big merchant ships coming down the Sound of Mull

The *Lochearn* with a 'selection of passengers', including crofters and cattle. (Murray)

*'At Oban I went to the quayside to board a boat to take us to Tiree. I was rather surprised to find we had to share our accommodation with a load of cows and sheep. Somewhere off the coast of Ardnamurchan the legs of the cows and sheep were tied together and the bound animals were hoisted over the side, into open boats to be rowed ashore.'* WH Smith.

and heading out towards the open sea. They were mostly American Liberty ships and were escorted by one or two corvettes, which were busy flashing out messages on their signal lamps. We watched them until the last ship disappeared into the dusk. Never to be forgotten.'

Frank Hamp also has recollections of this journey. 'Tobermory was a small harbour, which our captain entered with great care. As we did so my attention was drawn to the

Members of crew on board a MacBraynes ferry, in the Sound of Mull. (Campbell)

'Sailing to Tiree, we called at Salen. Most of the inhabitants seem to have come out to welcome us. The crew and passengers called out loud greetings to those on shore in the Gaelic. The captain gave a blast on his whistle and we steamed slowly away from the jetty, to continue our journey up the Sound.' Frank Hamp.

Rowing boat with passengers setting out to meet a MacBraynes ferry from Oban. (Murray)

'At Kilchoan there was no jetty. A small boat appeared, threading its way through a sizeable colony of seals. A funeral party stepped quietly down into it, followed by the coffin of a Highlander going home to his or her eternal rest. In the depths of our boat an unseen piper began to play, the mournful notes of his lament accompanying the party across the water, until the coffin had been brought safely ashore.' Frank Hamp.

bold lettering on the sea-wall proclaiming to the world that "God is love". It was so blunt, so Scottish! It left no room for doubt. At Tobermory the gangplank was lowered and a small tide of Mull people, with their cattle and sheep, flowed across – the bellowing and bleating showing that the animals, at least, were glad to feel solid ground beneath their feet once more.

'Beyond Kilchoan we met the full Atlantic swell, with long, lazy rollers spilling over the bows of the boat. Far back down the Sound I had been hearing muffled thuds, which I had taken to be a thunderstorm. I was wrong. On our starboard beam a sleek, grey destroyer appeared suddenly from behind Ardnamurchan Point, and it began firing its guns. It was a bad moment! But fortunately it passed when I saw the white ensign

The *Clydesdale* being loaded at Scarinish pier, during WW2, while one RAF man puts in a spot of fishing. (Dimond)

*'Christmas of 1943 I managed with luck to get leave. There was a terrific storm, we were informed that the ferry would run alongside the pier and the people who were prepared to jump on could do so. So the ferry passed, I jumped onto the deck. But the boat anchored in the bay. I sat bruised in a chair all night and the next morning, under a blue sky, the ferry docked at the pier and all the passengers boarded in the normal manner.'* George Cooper.

fluttering in the breeze and a large target being towed along by a tug on our port side. A target already bracketed by towering water-spouts! We were blithely heading for the gap between the two and I confidently expected the warship's commander to cease firing. He did no such thing, and I held my breath as we steamed on with the shells whistling overhead.

'The twin humps of Coll and Tiree had appeared on the horizon and, as if to greet the sight, the sun slid out from behind the clouds and brought out all the colours in the sea; from the green on one side of us to a deep blue on the other. Disporting themselves in this marine paradise were hundreds of jellyfish. I had entered another world.'

CHAPTER 15

# RAF Tiree in the Post-War Period

A fter the war ended there was a small RAF presence and then a temporary lull in the 'military occupation' of the island. However, by the 1950s the 'Cold War' was in full swing and, once more, it seemed that Tiree and other western islands on Europe's fringe could become the frontline of another destructive conflict.

Andrew Stewart recalls. 'I served for a few months in 1946 on Tiree (Kilkenneth) as a radar operator on a "care and maintenance" basis. Radar was still top secret and cameras forbidden at the time. It was great at Kilkenneth, as there were only four of us there. The radar station was off the air. There was more activity at the airfield, from where we drew our rations and supplies. Even though the war was over and Hitler gone, the radar equipment had to be kept warm and dry and the beacons lit at night on the aerials. I studied in my spare time and took the War Educational Certificate while there. I remember having supper at a couple of crofts and noticing the ex-RAF pots, pans and lino, which was being put to good use. It was a sad time in a way – the war was over and there was better excitement around operational stations.'

Roy Smith also experienced these times. 'I was stationed at Tiree from May to August 1946, as a "store basher" [an equipment assistant]. I was part of a "care and maintenance party". At Tiree we were closing down and packing up. The commanding officer was Squadron Leader Preston Potts who I heard built a boat out of RAF equipment. I had been a sergeant wireless operator/air gunner, and was compulsorily re-mustered to a ground trade in July 1945, just after the end of the war in Europe. We resented and did not understand this.

'Our Sergeant "Chiefy" Lodge told me when he left Tiree that he and Sergeant "Cookie" Alexander had been the last two servicemen left on the Island. His ambition was to visit or live on Tiree one day. He had, I think, spent most of the war there. He told me tremendous stories about the winds during the winter. "Chiefy" Lodge told me that a lot of valuable and important equipment would be left behind because it was not practical to dismantle it, and it was surplus to requirements.

'I spent three interesting months in idyllic weather on Tiree. One evening I went for a cycle ride to somewhere I had never been before, or since. There were former RAF wooden huts standing empty, with doors open. Cattle had been wandering in and out of the huts and cow dung was everywhere.'

In the 1950s the government decided 'early warning' systems were required, and many WW2 radar locations were deemed appropriate sites for 'ROTOR' [radar stations with upgraded electronic installations]. New buildings went up on Ben Gott and the nearby Balephetrish Hill. However, the rapid technological advances of the decade led to Master Radar Stations, covering a greater geographic area, being preferred. Some of the smaller stations, such as Tiree, were therefore redundant a relatively short time after their construction.

Brian Linnell's RAF service took him to a number of Hebridean radar sites during 1954–6. 'ROTOR 1 sites were planned to be between 50 and 80 miles apart. I remember sites in west Scotland at Kilchiaran (Islay), Aird Uig (Lewis), Saxa Vord (Unst), Scarinish (Tiree) and Cape Wrath (Durness). The sites included a concrete bunker with 50 to 100 men or women posted at different times. The prevailing winds on the islands meant certain aerials could not be used.'

Dennis Anderson wrote, 'I was a National Serviceman with the RAF, stationed on Tiree for a short time during the height of the Cold War in the mid-fifties. I was doing my National Service at a radar station in the East Neuk of Fife – 315 Signals Unit, RAF Anstruther, (better known now as Scotland's Secret Underground Bunker). The threat of east-west relations breaking down and NATO finding itself in direct opposition to the Warsaw Pact countries, was secondary to a threat posed by our Sergeant Lowe; "If you don't behave you'll find yourself posted to Tiree." Nobody knew where Tiree was, but he said it with such venom that we were led to believe it must be the end of the world!

'Early in 1956 a group of about eight airmen, consisting of one officer, one NCO, two fighter plotters, three radar operators and including at least one radar technician, found ourselves "posted to Tiree". I was among the defaulters!

'We were transported from RAF Anstruther to the nearby former Royal Naval Air Station at Crail, where we boarded an ancient RAF Avro Anson aircraft. Landing at Tiree we noticed the runway had been allowed to fall into disrepair. Some months before our

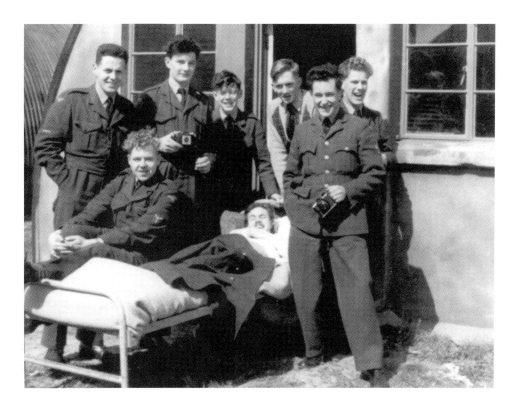

Dennis Anderson and friends outside their Nissen hut, during 1950s National Service on Tiree. (Anderson)

*'On National Service pay we couldn't afford to go drinking every night. As the weather then was lovely, some of us would go for a walk to the nearest beach.'* Dennis Anderson.

arrival a Hawker Hunter from RAF Leuchars had made an emergency landing on Tiree and promptly burst a tyre. While at RAF Scarinish there was a lot of reconstruction work being undertaken by civilian contractors on the runway. This may have been the result of the Hunter incident, or the increased "Cold War" importance of Tiree.

'The majority of RAF radar stations in the mid-fifties were in the east coast of the UK. In 1956 the Warsaw Pact countries regularly flew missions over the North Sea to test the RAF response times for interceptions. The introduction of long-range Russian aircraft incursions meant that an additional watch had to be kept on our "back door", the Atlantic – hence the upgrading of Tiree.

'Scarinish Operations Room was a large house. At RAF Scarinish there wasn't a NAAFI but there was a canteen which sold beer. As the commanding officer of the station at that time was Fl. Lt Bull, the canteen was called the "Bull Inn". I remember some of the civilian workers would join us. Also, two American Air Force servicemen would turn up regularly – so the Americans must have been involved in bolting the UK's "back door" in the 1950s.

'Tiree, a lovely place, unspoiled in 1956. Despite Sergeant Lowe's threat we all thoroughly enjoyed ourselves. The food was great. Perhaps that was because the cookhouse was catering for the civilian construction workers too. They would complain, whereas the "squaddies" couldn't. With little or no employment that I could see, times must have been hard. When we travelled from the domestic site to the operations block we saw, and had sympathy for, a family of "travelling people" with a broken down caravan thing, with matching horse and dear knows how many bairns. How they survived I'll never know.'

'Survive' they may well have done, as Tiree has successfully survived many fluctuating 'invasions' and fashions over the decades.

CHAPTER 16

# The Legacy of War

The official end of the war in Europe, 8 May 1945, was celebrated on Tiree. 'I remember the day the war finished as well. We got up here as normal, going to school down the road. And at Neil Johnston's there was a big red ensign on a bamboo fishing rod. He'd heard the news. We didn't have a radio. It would be about half nine in the morning because school went in at ten o'clock in these days. So actually it was Neil Johnston's uncle who came out and met me, and Neil was with him because he was at school with me. "Do about turn!" he says. "No school today! Go home and tell your mother the war's over!" That's how I knew the war had ended. There were big bonfires all round the island, and the RAF boys were letting off shots. Everybody was happy and celebrations and that. Tiree was dry in them days, there was no drink or nothing, except the lads at the NAAFI. I remember up by the [Baugh] monument there was a big bonfire there.' Hugh MacKinnon, Baugh

Leo Crowther, from 280 Squadron, also remembers that day. 'When VE [Victory in Europe] Day finally arrived, the islanders and ourselves erupted with joy and not a little sadness for the friends we had said goodbye to, and who would never return. The VE night celebrations in the Sergeants' Mess were part planned and part impromptu, with drinking, dating, singing and dancing escalating to riotous proportions.'

The base did not close straight away, as he remembers. The war in the far east suddenly seemed a long way away, but the news was followed closely. 'We had resumed regular flying patrols but expected to be posted to somewhere in the Far East theatre of war. In fact we had been given our injections for that very purpose. However, on what was to prove our last operational flight from Tiree during the first week of August, we were up before dawn, briefed and on our way to our aircraft, when someone on the truck taking us there mentioned that the US Air Force had dropped an atom bomb on Hiroshima. I can remember very clearly that a cold feeling of apprehension went through me, and the certain knowledge that mankind had unleashed the most terrifying force the world had ever seen.

'Eventually came the call to another posting. We had become part of the fabric of the tiny island of Tiree; wild as it was at times but a peaceful and lovely place during the warm sunny summers of 1944 and 1945. I even feel a touch of affection for the MacBrayne's steamships of those long gone days, chugging along to Mull and all points west. What can I say about the civilian population? Admiration, for their flexibility in accepting and coping with the advent of these RAF "bods" arriving in their midst; showing us the quiet courtesy and friendship which is still apparent.'

The RAF was determined that nothing of value would be left after the war, and islanders played a game of cat and mouse with the authorities.

'After the war there was lovely lino in the huts. People went at night and lifted that -it was going to be burnt. There were lovely new buckets and they [the RAF] just got a pick through them, and I think they were buried at *Tràigh Bhàigh* [in the dunes at Crossapol Beach]. Some people got into trouble. The police went to this house – it was just a father and a daughter. They were questioning them. "No, they didn't have anything." Then the daughter said in Gaelic, "*An innis dhaibh de tha ann an lobhta?*" ["Shall we tell them what is in the loft?"]. Unfortunately for them the policeman spoke Gaelic too! When they all went away we used to go through the huts and take down the pin-ups from the cubicles.' Mairi Campbell, *Corrairigh*

Tiree was never to be the same again. At times over 2,000 servicemen and women had shared their 'outpost' with the 1,500 islanders, who called it their home. The small island had been brought crashing into the twentieth century in five intense, tumultuous years.

'It's a terrible thing to say but there were lots of things that came with the war. We didn't feel the horror of war. Everything was just plentiful, different things that we hadn't been able to get.' Mairi Campbell, *Corrairigh*

A Gaelic-speaking community would be left with English as its main language. Gravel tracks became tarmacadamed roads, with one islander later remarking that, 'Hitler was the best councillor Tiree ever had!' Most of the camp buildings were demolished, but a number found a new life; the Sergeants' Mess in Crossapol becoming the Community Hall. The huge, three-runway aerodrome, out of all proportion to the rest of the island, is still in use and has significantly improved communications with Glasgow.

AIRPORT CONTROL TOWER, ISLE OF TIREE

The Control Tower built as part of RAF Tiree. This building was demolished in the 1990s. Today, a few dogged architectural remnants of WW2 can still be seen, dotted around the island. To some, they add a poignant note to the island's charm.

Of course the most significant change on Tiree after the war was the return of those islanders, changed utterly by their experiences, who had served away – and the terrible emptiness left by those who did not return. Two-thirds of the adult male population of Tiree – 202 – are listed in the Roll of Honour for service during the Second World War, while the War Memorial overlooking Gott Bay lists 32 men who died, 16 of whom served in the Merchant Navy. Several women from the island had also served.

For those taking their leave of the Services and this island posting, what next? Some viewed Britain as a 'tired, old country'; too many good young men and women having perished in two world wars. Emigrating was a possible option. What awaited those who remained; up to eight more years of rationing, but a National Health Service and 'prefab' housing. Looking back, perhaps a few asked, were the sacrifices worthwhile?

However, after the certainties of war, the most poignant epitaph comes from Hugh MacLean, Barrapol:

'Do you know this? The ones we looked upon as our enemies – I met one or two of them. And there was one in particular, what a gentleman! A German. And he opened his heart to me. That was years after the war. The time the ferry, *Loch Seaforth*, sunk at the pier over there [in 1971]. They had to get a salvage vessel from the continent to pick her up. One of the crew, I met him at a dance, what a gentleman. I remember, we were sitting in the committee room, we had our uniform on – we were in the pipe band, you see. I was sitting there and the rest of the boys were around, and this fellow came in and there was an empty seat, and he approached me. "May I sit?" he asked. "Yes, you're very welcome," I said. He had this smile on his face. He'd be about my own age at that time. And he turned round eventually. "I suppose," he said – his English was a wee bit broken but still he was very good just the same – "I suppose," he said, "You and I fought one another in the war."

"Oh!" I said, "You're German."

"Yes," he says, "I'm German." Now it was a German crew they had aboard that vessel.

"No," I said, "I wasn't in the armed forces [Hugh had been in a Protected Occupation as a farmer during the war]. Maybe I fought you in some other way, producing food." And he opened his heart to me.

"What's wrong?" he says. "We're the same people. Why does this happen?" he says. Oh! What a nice chap. He was from Holstein, in the east part of Germany, at the foot of Denmark. And he was praising our music. "It's like the music," he says, "that I'm used to in my own homeland." And he stayed with me there, and I enjoyed his conversation. A very nice fellow. And eventually he said, "Would you excuse me, I'd like to go out. I'll be back to see you," he said, "but I'd like to go out at the moment." And when he came back we were playing the pipes for the audience, and we went back to where we were in the committee room, and he walked in with a big bottle of good whisky on him and put it on the table in front of us. "That's from me," he says "to the boys."

"Oh!" I said. "Thank you very much," I said. "We didn't expect that."

"Well, it's the least I can do. I enjoyed your conversation." He was a very nice fellow, a German. And we were taught to hate these men!'

# Wartime in Tiree

DONALD S. MURRAY

The scythe and ploughshare would have stilled
during work of seed or harvest
when islanders peered to see steel
wings soaring, falling, coasting home from east or west,

or when they could hear a mingling of voices,
their conversation hushed and awed
by sounds of Polish, Czech, Italian,
the clank of machinery when fine, broad

roads were laid down; foundations of shelters
dug deep upon the machair; fields
that no longer yielded long grass or grain
but instead bore stooks of rifles, ack-ack guns arranged

to defend their empty acres. They watched loud airmen drive
cattle home, steer a stubborn shorthorn with bare hands
as if it were a burning Halifax
they were coaxing – very slowly – towards land

through skies clouded by flocks of smoke or sheep.
They saw, too, hangars swallow houses, barns,
mines wedged tight on rock by spindrift,
ticking with a cargo of both true and false alarm.

And this happened during days of whispers,
those secret years when wake of planes
trailed waves and eddies on their grazing,
the vapour-trails of ghosts who will not haunt these shores again,

whose presence troubled heart and nerve of islanders,
shook ears of oats and barley grain.

Donald S. Murray, born in 1956, teaches in Shetland. A Gaelic speaker, he comes from Ness in Lewis, with family connections to Balemartine, Tiree. His books include *The Guga Hunters*; *And on This Rock*; *Between Minch and Muckle Flugga*; *Small Expectations*; *Speak to Us, Catriona* and *Weaving Songs*.

'We used to walk down the strand to the hamlet of Balemartine to buy eggs, which we cooked on the stove of our hut. On rare occasions you could smell kippers cooking. Sometimes we attempted a short cut from the road across rough ground, to the hangars and Flight Offices. If it was the nesting season we would be attacked by terns; they were quite fearless and would dive down and knock one's hat off. There were many other resident sea-birds and waders, these included oystercatchers, terns, dunlin, curlew and snipe.' Peter Rackliff, 518 Squadron. (Gill)

WAAF Greta Trevers, who had served at Tiree, made a sentimental, brief return visit in 2009 and lovingly gathered some pebbles on the beach. She sent one to the Natural History Museum for analysis and their reply said these samples are among the oldest rocks in Europe.

# Glossary and Abbreviations

AC1 – Aircraftman, 1st Class

AC2 – Aircraftman, 2nd Class

AFC – Air Force Cross (award)

ASDIC – Allied Submarine Detection Investigation Committee (early form of sonar)

ASR – Air Sea Rescue

ATS – Auxiliary Territorial Service (Women's armed service)

Bismuth/Mercer – code names for RAF meteorological flights

Bods – short for bodies (extra hands)

Carley float – a life raft designed by American inventor Horace Carley

CO – Commanding Officer

Compass Adjuster – RAF trade; aircraft were 'swung' to calibrate compasses

D-day – the code name for the date of the invasion of France, 6 June 1944

DF – Direction Finding

DFC – Distinguished Flying Cross

DH – De Havilland (aircraft manufacturer)

D Notice – censorship notice to prevent publication of information relating to national security

ENSA – Entertainments National Service Association

'erks' – slang for aircraftman (lower ranks)

EU – embarkation unit

Fitter – engineering repair/maintenance

Fl Lt – Flight Lieutenant

FO – Flying Officer

HMS – Her (His) Majesty's Ship

HQ – Headquarters

Jock's Box – nickname for Church of Scotland tea bars, often located on railway platforms

LAC – Leading Aircraftman

LACW – Leading Aircraft Woman

Lt Cmdr – Lieutenant Commander

Met – short for meteorology/meteorological

MO – Medical Officer

MT – Motor Transport

MTB – Motor Torpedo Boat

NAAFI – Navy, Army and Air Force Institutes (canteen/shop)

NCO – Non Commissioned Officer

OBE – Officer of (the Order of) the British Empire (honorary award)

OC – Officer Commanding

op(s) – short for operational (active service) missions/flights

PO Prune – wartime nickname for bumptious, accident-prone officer

POW – Prisoner(s) of War

RAF – Royal Air Force

RAAF – Royal Australian Air Force

RCAF – Royal Canadian Air Force

RNR – Royal Naval Reserve

sortie – operational flight (not training)

snoek – collective term for 'unusual' wartime seafood, including whale

Sqn – Squadron

Sqn Ldr – Squadron Leader

SS – Steam Ship

USAAF – United States Army Air Force

USS – United States Ship (or Steamer)

VE Day – 8 May 1945 when hostilities in Europe in World War II officially ceased

VHF – Very High Frequency

VIP – Very Important Person

VJ Day – Victory over Japan when hostilities in World War II against Japan officially ceased

WAAF – Women's Auxiliary Air Force

Wing Co – Wing Commander

Wop/AG – Wireless operator – Air gunner

WRNS – Women's Royal Naval Service

WW1 – World War I

WW2 – World War II

# Acknowledgements

Airmail Magazine, D Anderson, R Anderson, M Angell, An Iodhlann, J Ankerson, A Ashcroft, A Atkins, A Jeziorski, D Atkinson, R Aylott, J Ayres, T Bacon, S Bagley, G Bainbridge, A Barton, N Beale, J Bell, S Berlie, R Bishop, R Blaber, J Bowler, P Bridge, A Bridgwater, M Briengan, M Briscoe, T Brock, I Brown, N Brownlie, H Bryce, L Burden, A Campbell, C Campbell, G Campbell, M Campbell, R Campbell, W Campbell, R Card, B Cass, M Chaffe, B Chambers, M Chilton, B Clark, I Clark, P Clark, D Cobb, L Cobb, D Collison, G Cooper, J Creal, L Crowther, T Currie, S Davis, T Dimond, W Dimond, C Drabble, S Duncan, D Eastwood, P Eiles, J Entwistle, J Evans (Paterchurch Publications), A Faulkner, C Fisher, C Forbes, M Foster, J Fowler, D Fox, M Fraser, L Frewer, A Gallier, F Gee, M Gibson, O Gill, M Goold, L Gowans, J Graham, D Grant, J Green, C Gunn, J Hall, R Hall, C Hallett, G Hambling, F Hamp, B Hanson, J Harper, B Harris, R Harris, E Harrison, A Hendrie, G Holleyman, F Holmes, Professor M Howe, R Howie, G Howlett, J Hughes, J Hurst, D Humphreys, H Hunter, J Hunter, J Inglis, B Jamieson, F Jenkins, N Johnston, P Jones, A Keeling, K Kennedy, N Kennedy, E Kerrigan, V King, F Krzyszczuk, A Lacy, L Lambert, J Legg, B Lewis, J Liddy, B Linnell, E Lotocka, K Lunn, A MacDonald (amdphoto.co.uk), E MacDonald, A MacEachan, D MacFarlane, A MacLean, D MacLean, H MacLean, J G MacLean, N A MacLean, S MacLean, H MacLeod, H MacPhail, D MacPhee, M McArthur, D McClounnan, D McCusker, D McKinnon, H McKinnon, J McKinnon, M McKinnon, N Mason, R Massey, C Moffat, D Morrison, N Morrison, J Mowbray, A Munn, N Munn, D Murray, W Nash, E Nelson, J Newman, E Nichols, J Nielson, Oban Times (K Campbell), C Oldfield, L Olsen, H Parker, J Parrish, C Paterson, E Peacock, G Pearman, S Pelling, Polish Museum and Sikorski Institute [W DeLuga, A Jeziorski, Capt Milewski, M Olizar], G Porazka, P Rackcliff, R Radford, V Radford, R Roberts, K Salt, J Shepherd, N Short, A Sinclair, W Singleton, P Sloman, H Smith, R Smith, W Smith, D Snow, Z Solecki, R Spinks, D Springett, H Springett, A Stewart, J Stewart, K Stoker, D Suckling, J Sylvester, T Teague, F Thorn, R Toy, G Traub, G Trevers, M Tuckwell, A Twelvetrees, P Wakelin, K Walker, K Waller, R Watson, B Weatherill, D Wheeley, E Wheeley, P Whitworth, F Williams, P Williams, J Wilson, T Wilson, E Wise, D Withers, C Woodcock (Blue Beyond), Professor E Zarudzki, E Ziomek, S Ziomek.

## Mike Hughes

Growing up in the 1960s, Mike was surrounded by family who served in World War Two. His father volunteered for the Royal Navy aged seventeen and an uncle was killed serving in the RAF. Mike devoured every comic and book he could on WW2, and considered writing as a hobby for many years.

Mike's wife Barbara's mother is from Tiree and her father from Taynuilt, by Oban. Mike and Barbara moved from Lanarkshire to live and work in Oban and Argyll from 1988 to 1998. Being fascinated by the legacy of WW2, still evident in ageing buildings and in people's recollections, and finding little or nothing in print on this area's contribution to the war effort, Mike had his subject and a cause to fulfil the writing ambition. It is almost twenty years since he set out tentatively seeking memories of those who served in this area during the War. He gave talks and slideshows and assisted with establishing and encouraging local museums to feature WW2. He has published two previous books; *Hebrides at War*, Birlinn, 1998 and *Stornoway in WW2*, Islands Book Trust, 2008 and has also written an introduction to the re-published *Tartan Pimpernel*, Birlinn, 1999, and contributed to *Island Heroes*, Islands Book Trust, 2009. During this time Mike has written articles for a wide range of newspapers and magazines including *The Oban Times*, *Scottish Memories* and *Scottish Island Explorer*.

Mike has amassed an enormous collection of first-hand accounts of life during WW2 and photographs relating to all districts in west and north Scotland. Mike has worked on a number of radio and TV programmes for Oban FM initially, then BBC Radio and TV Scotland, Radio 4, STV. Some of these programmes were made in partnership with Tiree's well-known broadcaster and singer Mary Ann Kennedy. The Hughes family made and still have many good friends in Oban and on the islands. Mike met Dr John Holliday through their mutual love of island history and John asked Mike to give talks on the Island of Tiree including the Feis Lecture in 1999.

Mike had over twenty years' experience working in vocational guidance and project management before becoming a teacher in 2002. He is Principal Teacher of Religious Education in Bishopbriggs. Barbara and Mike have five children. They visit the west highlands and Hebrides at every opportunity. Historical research comes a close third after family and rugby for Mike.

## Dr John Holliday

John Holliday has been the doctor on Tiree since 1986. He previously worked for the aboriginal health service of the Pintupi people in Australia's Western Desert, where he worked closely with the *ngangkari*, or traditional healer.

Originally from Norfolk, he has family connections with the Channel Islands and Shetland, including a Gaelic-speaking great, great, great grandmother from Kilmorack, near Beauly. He is chair of *An Iodhlann*, Tiree's historical centre and archive, and also *Fèis Thiriodh*, the island's traditional music festival. Having learned Gaelic, he has spent years soaking up the place names and stories from the island's tradition bearers and has made a number of oral history recordings for the archive. He wrote *Island of Two Harvests* for *An Iodhlann* in 2006. His song *Spirit of the Land* was recorded in 1999 as part of the Songhunter competition and he also has tunes published in the *Nineties Collection*.